Finding a Way Out

Finding a Way Out

*The Inspiring Story of a Life Devoted to
Freedom, Opportunity and Justice in America*

Robert Moton
Edited by Paul Dennis Sporer

Bylany Press

Anza Publishing, Chester, NY 10918
Bylany Press is an imprint of Anza Publishing
Copyright © 2005 by Anza Publishing

This work is a new, unabridged edition of *Finding a Way Out: An Autobiography* by Robert Russa Moton, originally published in 1921.

Library of Congress Cataloguing-in-Publication Data
Moton, Robert Russa, 1867-1940.
   Finding a way out / Robert Moton ; edited by Paul Dennis Sporer.
      p.   cm.
   Includes index.
   ISBN 1-932490-18-3 (hardcover: alk. paper)
   1. Moton, Robert Russa, 1867-1940.
   2. African Americans — Biography.
   3. African American educators — Biography.
   4. Educators — United States — Biography.
   5. Tuskegee Institute — Biography.
   6. African Americans — Social conditions-to 1964.
I. Sporer, Paul D. II. Title.
E185.97.M9 2005
370'.92—dc22   2005021082

All rights reserved. No part of this publication may be reproduced, stored in a retrieval system, or transmitted, in any form or by any means, electronic, mechanical, photocopying, recording or otherwise, without the prior permission of the copyright holder.

Visit AnzaPublishing.com for more information on outstanding authors and titles. Please support our efforts to restore great literature to a place of prominence in our culture.

ISBN: 1-932490-18-3 (hardcover)

∞ This book is printed on acid-free paper.

CONTENTS

	Editor's Preface	*i*
1	Out of Africa	1
2	On A Virginia Plantation	7
3	Through Reconstruction	17
4	Doing and Learning	22
5	A Touch of Real Life	34
6	Ending Student Days	46
7	Black, White, and Red	53
8	With North and South	68
9	From Hampton to Tuskegee	84
10	At Tuskegee	94
11	War Activities	107
12	Forward Movements in the South	122
	Index	*133*

Editor's Preface

This highly engaging book by Robert Moton is the memoir of a respected black educator and a tireless promoter of racial harmony. It provides a unique and valuable perspective of the social environment in the United States, from the Reconstruction period, to the years following World War I. Also described are the critical changes in culture that gave blacks the opportunity to attain higher education and social rank.

However, what makes this memoir especially enlightening is its depiction of the series of events that Moton experienced in his struggle to achieve a prestigious role in society. He recounts his childhood living in extreme poverty, and the long road of building up his mental and moral character, while assuming increasingly important positions of authority. He reached his zenith when he took up the leadership of the Tuskegee Institute after Booker T. Washington, and he was the one chiefly responsible for establishing the famous hospital for black war veterans. Moton's book could justifiably be called a detailed record of a great "success story"; his objective and balanced writing gives us an inside look as to how this transformation, from the poor son of emancipated slaves to esteemed advisor to Presidents, actually took place.

Although it is a truism to say that no two life stories are exactly the same, when it comes to the lives of successful people, certain key events, breakthroughs or turning points are commonly seen. Of crucial importance are those influential individuals ready to offer assistance in navigating the difficult "forks in the road". This chronicle is not only interesting and instructive, but inspirational, especially for young people, demonstrating the value of education, discipline, hard work, and cooperation.

The present work is a new, unabridged edition of *Finding a Way Out: An Autobiography*, originally published in 1921, by Doubleday, Page & Co. Restoration was straightforward. We have in general preserved the original text, while correcting the spelling of certain words, and adjusting or adding punctuation where necessary. We have also added an index.

Paul Dennis Sporer

Chapter 1

Out of Africa

ABOUT the year 1735 a fierce battle was waged between two strong tribes on the west coast of Africa. The chief of one of these tribes was counted among the most powerful of his time. This chief overpowered his rival and slaughtered and captured a great number of his band. Some of the captives escaped, others died, others still committed suicide, till but few were left. The victorious chief delivered to his son about a dozen of this forlorn remnant, and he, with an escort, took them away to be sold into slavery. The young African pushed his way through the jungle with his bodyguard until he reached the coast. Arrived there, he sold his captives to the captain of an American slave ship and received his pay in trinkets of various kinds, common to the custom of the trade. Then he was asked to row out in a boat and inspect the wonderful ship. He went, and with the captain and the crew saw every part of the vessel. When it was all over they offered him food and he ate it heartily. After that, he remembered no more till he woke to find himself in the hold of the ship chained to one of the miserable creatures whom he himself had so recently sold as a slave, and the vessel itself was far beyond the sight of land.

After many days the ship arrived at the shores of America; the human cargo was brought to Richmond and this African slave merchant was sold along with his captives at public auction in the slave markets of the city. He was bought by a tobacco planter and carried to Amelia County, Virginia, where he lived to be a very old man. This man was my grandmother's great-grandfather.

According to the story as he told it to my grandmother, he brought more at auction than any other member of the party. He was a very fine specimen of physical manhood, weighing somewhere around two hundred pounds, and standing about six feet two inches in height. My grandmother said of him that he learned very little of the English language and used what little he knew always with a pronounced foreign accent. He never grew to like America or Americans, white or black; and certain days, after the passing of so many moons, he observed religiously throughout his life. These were feast days with certain ceremonies of their own, in which, when possible, two other members of that same party though not of his tribe would join him. Each understood the tribal language of the others. These days, so my grandmother said, which occurred about three times a year, his owner permitted him to take off, leaving him undisturbed, for at other times he was entirely faithful and conscientious in his work. His great-granddaughter — my mother's mother — was not, I should judge, very unlike this great-great-great-grandfather of mine, for in her youth she was a magnificent type of womanhood, both physically and mentally; and even to her death, at ninety-six years of age, she was possessed of remarkable physical and mental vigour. She "carried the keys" on her owner's, Doctor Craddock's, plantation, and stood next on the female side of the household to his wife, superintending the making of the clothes, caring for the children on the plantation, and in later years conducting what would in the present day be called a Day Nursery; that is, caring for the children of the mothers who were in the field, seeing to their food and dress, and to their conduct, of course. Frequently these old mothers were very clever in story telling, so that "Uncle Remus," "Brer Fox," and "Brer Rabbit" were familiar to the children of the South, both white and black, many years before they got into print.

My father's mother, who lived to be 108 years old, was also brought directly from Africa, and was finally sold to a planter who lived in Charlotte County, Virginia. It was there my father was born. He was owned by Doctor Alexander of that county, and when he died, about 1850, and the estate was divided, my father was sold to John Crowder of Prince Edward County, and, I think, presented to his wife as a Christmas present. I have many times heard my father tell of his experiences as a slave; of the many hardships through which he passed, and of the many good times he had even as a slave, for one of the fortunate traits of the Negro is his jovial nature, his ability to see humour even in adversity, and to laugh and sing under almost any circumstances. I have often thought that most other races, had they gone through the difficulties which the Negro faced, would have produced much more insanity than has been found in the past among Negroes; unfortunately, however, insanity is increasing very much indeed among my people, an indication in all probability that they are taking life much more seriously than they have done in the past.

There were many kind masters during slavery days; and there must have been such a thing as kindness even between master and slave. The overseers who were generally of the poorer class of white people were, as a rule, the cause of much of the contention and usually made most of the trouble; at least the Negroes thought so. They were night patrollers, or, as the Negroes called them, "patter-rollers," and were paid by the hour in many places to catch and whip any slave found off his master's plantation after nightfall without a pass. Not infrequently these people received from the master class less consideration even than the slave, and in most cases the bitterest animosity and hatred existed between the overseers and the slaves. It was not unusual that Negroes considered themselves superior in every respect to the overseer class, whose members were generally referred to among them as "po'h white trash." This expression was "the last word" in degradation, infamy, and general contempt that Negroes could command. Even today, when Negroes refer to people as "poor white trash," it has a meaning all its own, and I am of the opinion that much of the ill feeling between the races in our country today had its origin in these unpleasant relations between overseer and slaves before Emancipation.

On the Crowder plantation, there was an overseer who had a particular dislike for my father, probably because he thought that my father received entirely too much consideration from his master and mistress; in short, there was a kind of jealous rivalry between them. It is unnecessary to say that the dislike on the part of the overseer was generously reciprocated by my father. If there was any difference, it was that the hatred on my father's part was the stronger—if that were possible; and without doubt, being in the confidence of his master, he used his opportunity to the disadvantage of the overseer. It was the rule of the plantation that no slaves except such as the master designated should be whipped by the overseer. My father, of course, was thus exempted. On one occasion the overseer, unfortunately, and against the order of his employer, insisted upon whipping my father. The scene took place in a tobacco barn where my father was engaged with perhaps fifty other slaves in sorting and stripping tobacco. In the scuffle, in which several other slaves helped the overseer in response to his call, my father easily got the upper hand, for he was a man of unusual strength. He not only overpowered the overseer but the men who undertook to assist him, maiming the overseer and one of the men very seriously. This was in the midst of a severe snow storm. My father took the only course, as it seemed, that was open to "obstreperous" slaves—he took to the woods. This was in early December. Here he remained, picking up what food he could at nights in cabins and elsewhere, until March, when, for want of food and sufficient clothing, his feet having been frost bitten, he was obliged to give in. He returned one snowy afternoon, slipped into the stable, and hid himself in the loft under the hay. His hat was discovered by his master's two sons whose conversation, which he overheard, showed that they were afraid of him. They ran to the house and told their father of his return, and he came out to the barn and urged him to come to the house and be looked after, for the entire family was really very fond of him. He was taken back to the house where his mistress, the mother of the two boys, treated him most kindly. Indeed, he said, they all wept over his pitiable condition. His feet were finally, but only after careful nursing for several months, in shape to permit him to resume his usual duties. He promised that he would not commit the same offense again, provided, however, no "po'h white trash" attempted again to whip him. He apologized to the overseer, and the two agreed that there would be no further trouble. But a few weeks afterward he went to his master and told him he was very sorry it was not possible for him to get along with that overseer and asked that his master sell him to a near-by planter, who had agreed to give him better treatment. This time it would appear that he and the master came very near the "parting of the ways." This seems strange, I know, but it was not infrequent that slaves of the more intelligent type would make definite arrangements with some near or distant planter to buy them; thus slaves very often picked their own masters. But in this case Mr. Crowder made it plain to him that they could get along; that he was unwilling to sell him; that he belonged especially to his mistress and that she depended on him. My father insisted, however, that the overseer be discharged. Whether his attitude in this case produced the desired result my father did not know, but in any case within a few weeks the objectionable overseer left and a new overseer took his place, who established better relations, not only as between himself and my father, but with the other slaves as well, in consequence of which the master got better and more efficient service with very much less friction.

From that time forward, my father lived pleasantly on the Crowder plantation, neither he nor the master nor the overseer breaking their mutual promise—my father's being that he would not fight again unless someone attempted to whip him; and the overseer's, that he would not attempt to whip him. My father used to say that one man could not chastise another, although two men might fight and one might get the better of the other. That idea was very strong in his mind.

When the Civil War broke out my father went with Mrs. Crowder's brother — Captain Womack of Cumberland County, Virginia, who was afterward Colonel Womack — into the fray as his "body servant." I think they would say "valet" today. He was with him during the first three years of that bitter struggle, suffering all the privations and hardships so familiar to those who know what the Southern Army endured.

One experience he used often to relate was that near Petersburg, he accidentally got within the Union lines and was told that he might remain with the Yankees if he so desired; but he told them that he could not do so at the time because he had given his definite promise that he would stand by Colonel Womack until the war was over. He could not break his promise. He had also sworn to see to it, so far as he could, that no harm came to his master and he felt that he would remain true to that pledge so long as Colonel Womack was equally true to his promises to him. I am told that the friendship between the two men, one black, one white, was very strong; that nothing ever separated them save Colonel Womack's death which, as I recall my father's account of it, occurred in one of the famous charges near Petersburg.

When the war was over my father "hired himself" to the Crowders, where he remained until Christmas of 1866 when he married my mother, Emily Brown. They were married in the old plantation house of the Hillmans of Amelia County. The Hillmans, as I recall, were Scottish Presbyterians, and like many other Southerners, they had lost everything during the war except their name and honour and the pride of aristocratic ancestry.

My mother, like her own mother, was a woman of very strong character in many ways, very much like my father. Among my early recollections is the fact that my mother frequently, after working in the field all day, would hurry us through the evening meal in order to get the cabin ready for the night school which met regularly in our simple home. I recall now the eagerness with which some twenty-five or thirty men and women struggled with their lessons, trying to learn to read and write while I was supposed to be asleep in my trundle bed, to which I had been hurried to make room for this little band of anxious, aspiring ex-slaves, some of whom came as far as six miles in order to take advantage of this rare opportunity which but a few years before had been denied them. The teacher of this night school was my mother's brother, who, in spite of the penalties attached, had learned to read and write from his young master, picking up here and there snatches of information while they played and worked together, ofttimes without the young master's realizing the gravity of his actions. All this took place but a few years after the close of the war and before any schools had been established for coloured or white children in that section. My mother was one of the most enthusiastic of the students, while my father, who was much older than my mother, although giving his unqualified approval and encouragement to the school, sat by and listened and once in a while in a mischievous mood threw in an ejaculation which upset the order and dignity of the school, much to the embarrassment and annoyance of the teacher and, I fear, sometimes to the indignation of the more serious-minded students, especially my mother.

Thinking of the experiences through which my ancestors passed, along with thousands of other slaves, in their contact with the white people of America, I have often felt that somehow—in spite of the hardships and oppression which they suffered—that in the providence of God, the Negro, when all is summed up dispassionately, has come through the ordeal with much to his credit, and with a great many advantages over his condition when he entered the relationship. The white man, on the other hand, has reaped certain disadvantages from which the whole country still suffers, and from which it will in all likelihood take several generations to recover completely.

Chapter 2

On A Virginia Plantation

IN JANUARY, 1867, my father hired himself to Mr. Samuel Vaughan of Prince Edward County, and was made foreman or "head man" on the Vaughan plantation while his family continued to live in Amelia County. It was in Amelia County that I was born on the 26th day of August of the same year. Among my earliest recollections is one of my father appearing on a Saturday morning with a team of four mules hitched to a large farm wagon in charge of a coloured man, Beverley Jones, who rode one of the mules. My father and my mother, assisted by friends, packed our few belongings into this wagon and took me with my mother to the Vaughan plantation in Prince Edward County where my father had been working. I remember perfectly the long drive and how they wrapped me in an old gray blanket and a blue military overcoat—which were very common in those days—in order to protect me from the bitter cold. Here in an old house, in the rear of a Virginia mansion known as "Pleasant Shade," I spent most of the years of my early youth. My mother for many years was cook, and my father "led the hands" on the plantation. It was here that I caught my first glimpses of real culture and got my first inspiration as to what I would like to be and something of what I would like to do.

On account of my parents' relation to the household, and because I was the only child near the "big house," I naturally received much attention from the Vaughan family. I can never forget Mrs. Vaughan—"Miss Lucy" we called her, as was the custom not only among the coloured people but among the white folks also—and her three daughters, Misses Patty, Jennie, and Mollie. I was soon big enough to carry Miss Lucy's key basket. This was considered a great honour for a small Negro boy before the war and immediately afterward. I felt the "dignity and responsibility" of my office. As I grew older my duties increased until I assisted her and her daughters in the care of the fowls, of which she had a great number—turkeys, geese, ducks, and a great many chickens. But proud as I was of these duties, I have never since so sincerely envied any one his position as I did Sam Reed, the general house boy and waiter in the family. Miss Lucy had promised me that when Sam was big enough he would be transferred to the farm, as was the custom, and I could have his place. Sam helped the cook, made all the fires, was in the "big house" much of the time, and generally wore "good clothes." He was a favourite on the plantation. Besides all this, Sam was a remarkable acrobat. He could turn somersaults, stand on his head, turn a cart wheel, go wheelbarrow fashion, and could perform what were to me many very wonderful acrobatic feats, in addition to being a wonderfully good reel and jig dancer and a remarkably fine singer. He must have inherited his ability to sing from his father, "Uncle Jim," who was a noted "shout singer" in the neighbourhood. Sam was not a "Christian" and so sang anything; and he did it very effectively. Under Sam's direction I practised many of his accomplishments, and with his careful tutelage became a close second. As a result, he and I were frequently called into the "big house" to perform. But there was one thing I had against Sam. He grew so slowly it seemed that I would soon be bigger than he, and would lose my chance to get his place when he should be sent on to another. Fortunately for me, but perhaps unfortunately for Sam, his father now insisted that it was time for him to leave the house, as he considered him too old to devote himself to "doing chores"; and being only a house boy, his pay was too small. He would earn more by working on the farm. So Sam had to go.

I never shall forget the joy I felt when told that I was to wait on the table at breakfast the following morning, and how Sam and my mother instructed me until late in the night how to perform my new duties; how I should stand; and how to all appearances I was to pay no attention to the conversation. I remember how they sat at the table and had me pass things —empty plates and dishes—I do not recall whether from the right or left side, but judge now it must have been from the left. In any case, I got through my first day with some show of success and proved myself fairly equal to my new responsibilities. As a compliment to the honours of the post, the young ladies at the house made me a couple of suits which I should wear only on special occasions. I think I have never had a position since then in which I took any more pride than in this youthful promotion to the place to which I had aspired for several years. Yet there was more in my position than was at first apparent. "Mr. Willie" Vaughan, the only son, I took in many things as a model. I copied his laugh, his walk, his dress, the way he handled his knife and fork, and other characteristic manners of his in a fashion that must have sometimes amused those who observed me. But aside from its humorous aspects, this contact with the Vaughan family meant for me a certain kind of most valuable training and education.

About this time a rather interesting incident happened. While my work was new, my mother made me devote an hour at night to my blue backed Holmes's Primer. She was my teacher, being one of the very few coloured women in our neighbourhood who could read at all. There was a popular belief that the Vaughans, notwithstanding their kindness and aristocratic ideas, objected to and opposed Negroes' reading and writing. My mother was very careful, therefore, that they should not know that she was teaching me to read, or even that she herself could read. For several years she had kept from them the fact that she even knew one letter of the alphabet from another; but one night after the day's work was done there was a gentle rap at the door of our two roomed house. I remember that we were sitting before a big, open fire—my father, my mother, and I—my mother teaching me by the light from the fire. As the custom was in those days, my mother called out to learn who was there. Imagine our consternation when the answer came back: "Miss Lucy." My mother was tempted to hide the book when she discovered who was at the door, but my father objected, saying we were free and that he would leave the Vaughans if they made any objections; that he could find plenty of work at good pay at any one of a dozen plantations in the district. So the door was opened and in walked "Miss Lucy", to find us in the very act. She expressed the greatest surprise when she discovered what was taking place, but she astonished us equally when she indicated that she was very much pleased, and commended my mother on the fact that she could read and told her she was very wise to teach her son to read. The next day we were even more astonished and of course pleased when Miss Mollie, her youngest daughter, said to my mother that Mrs. Vaughan had asked her to give me a lesson for one hour every afternoon and to do the same for my mother if my mother would care to have her do so. So the next time my father went to Farmville, eight miles away, he bought the necessary books both for my mother and me, and my lessons began in a more systematic way with Miss Mollie as teacher and my mother as my "classmate" for one hour each afternoon. My mother finally dropped out but I continued for some time, though intermittently.

One of the saddest recollections of my childhood was the death of Mrs. Vaughan. I can never forget the impression it made upon me, the wailing of the coloured women on the plantation and the sadness of the coloured men. There must have been between three and four hundred people on the Vaughan estate, including men, women, and children.

Mrs. Vaughan, like her husband, possessed a very beautiful character and was beloved of everybody on the plantation. While I did not then appreciate the full gravity of the situation, I wept along with the others; for in spite of my youth I realized somewhat the loss that this death was to me as well as to others. For there was not a family on the plantation and scarcely a person who had not at some time been helped by her kindly personal attention to their needs and difficulties. Several years later Mr. Vaughan was married again — to Miss Pattie Perkinson, a daughter of Captain Perkinson, the head of another of Virginia's fine families, who owned a large estate a few miles away. I confess that I did not entirely approve of the marriage. The truth of the matter was I shared the feelings —perhaps in less degree—of most of the people on the plantation, especially the women; though my own feelings were more personal than general. I was not so worried about the marriage itself as I was anxious that whoever took "Miss Lucy's" place should not interfere with the position I was occupying in the Vaughan household. I was certain that no one could be so kind as "Miss Lucy" had been to me, and I felt sure that "Miss Pattie" would not be; and what I had heard of the dealings of certain members of her family with coloured people rather tended further to disquiet than to allay my youthful anxiety about my own future. My position at this time in the Vaughan household was, in my mind, of a very important sort. I was doing, so I supposed, just about as I wished, and running things much to my own liking. I carried the keys all day and hung them at the head of Mr. Vaughan's bed the last thing at night. I issued the corn for the stock and frequently helped in weighing the rations to the scores of men who came up Saturday afternoon for their allowances. I went hunting with Mr. Vaughan, visited the rabbit traps in the morning, and also went fishing with him on the Appomattox River. He rode a magnificent bay mare we called Fannie, while I rode a mule, blind in both eyes, named Kit. It is not surprising, therefore, that I should have been more or less jealous of my position and anxious that the new mistress of the house should be of a kind to meet my approval, for by this time the three daughters had all married and only Mr. Vaughan's son, Mr. William S. Vaughan, was left.

My mother was still the cook, and my father was running things as headman on the farm, but neither my father nor my mother counted very much in my mind so far as this situation was concerned; indeed Mr. Vaughan and his son did not count very much, looking at it from the mental angles of my youth. I was, however, very pleasantly surprised when "Miss Pattie" came to "Pleasant Shade." The things that had been prophesied regarding her were not fulfilled. She did not take the keys from me and I had just about as much leeway as before, in some respects more. She was more careful than the men folks had been about setting the table and cleaning the house, pulling up weeds, the clearing of the garden, and such things. She made me sweep off the porches once and sometimes twice or three times a day—I had gotten to the place where I swept them perhaps twice and sometimes only once a week. And besides all this, the new Mrs. Vaughan insisted that my mother should continue my lessons, and encouraged me in various other ways.

In the fall following this important event a school was opened for coloured children a few miles from the Vaughan plantation. This was the first school for Negroes in that neighbourhood; indeed the first school of any kind, for there had been no public schools of consequence for either white or coloured children before that time. In the fall of the previous year the coloured people had been urged to vote with the promise that if they did so a public school for their children would be established in our district. They voted according to instructions and the promise was kept.

In early October a free school was opened for coloured people, with Mr. John Morrisette, a white man, as teacher. My father and my mother decided that I should go. They consulted the Vaughans, particularly Mrs. Vaughan. She readily approved. Forthwith she and my mother fitted me out and I appeared in school the opening day. I recall how I felt when I observed that there were so many children bigger than myself who could not read. Because of my instruction at home I was in the highest class in the school. And I had special pride in the fact. I think I was reading in the third reader. But reading at all by a coloured boy in those days was rather unusual; and a coloured free school, with fifty or sixty children on the opening day, and meeting in the daytime as well, was a real marvel. Mr. Morrisette, who, by the way, had been an officer in the Southern Army, was most kind and thoughtful and very patient, and took a great deal of care and pains, even on the opening day, to classify us. He brought many books of various kinds, and his wife, who was a very unusual woman, came in later to help him in the difficult task of organizing this large number of Negro children into a real school. His task no doubt was a hard one, not only because of the children directly, but because of the parents as well, many of whom, as time went on, troubled him very much. All of us naturally thought the more books the student carried the more he knew, and many parents were therefore willing to get the fourth, fifth, and even the sixth reader for their children without any protest at the expense so long as they were carrying "bigger" and "higher" books. My father shared this feeling along with the rest. He was not altogether happy at my having only a third reader; but Mrs. Vaughan, who knew what I was doing, came to the rescue and assured him that I would have "bigger" books in ample time, and that I would probably learn more than many others who had many more books.

I continued my work in the Vaughan family, before and after school, at intervals for many years, and without doubt what I learned from my contact with them was worth quite as much to me as what I learned at school. Indeed, my own idea has always been that the one supplemented the other. My work before and after school was being correlated unconsciously with what I was learning in books; which was true also of my contact with the nearly four score children whom I met daily at school.

The Vaughans were of the finest type of Southern families — kind, thoughtful, and generous. They were people of considerable wealth and at the top of the social scale in that community; but at the same time they were of all the white people the most popular among the Negroes of the neighbourhood. They visited Negro churches and prayer meetings, and Negroes frequently visited the old Jamestown Presbyterian Church to which the Vaughans belonged and of which Mr. Vaughan, I think, was an elder, as was also his son in later years. For many years they conducted Sunday School in the afternoon at Jamestown Church for coloured people. This school was taught by the leading ladies of the community with the help of some of the leading white men. In this connection it is significant that the Vaughans never suffered for want of adequate and faithful help on the farm or in the household, and it is certain that their influence on the coloured people on their place and in that section was of the best. This was true of them in that day. It is equally true today of their three daughters and was true of their son and his wife, both of whom have died within the last few years. The Vaughans never lost any prestige or social standing in the community by being kind and helpful to coloured people.

The pastor of the Jamestown Presbyterian Church, to which I have referred, was the Rev. George H. Denney, a minister who lived in Amelia

County, some twenty miles away, and usually came to the community on Saturday afternoons in a sulky*. He generally made his home with the Vaughans, remaining over from Saturday until Monday. Occasionally he came earlier or remained later for certain special services. I was always glad to have him come, even though it added to my duties somewhat, because of the extra shoes to polish and the extra pail of water that I had to bring from the spring some distance away. At the same time he was very kind to me; it was he who gave me the first Bible that I ever had and took pains to interpret certain passages with which I had become somewhat familiar but whose meaning was as yet rather vague to me. But my joy at his coming lay in the fact that frequently, especially in the summer season, he brought with him his son George. He was of about my own age which accounted for our having many good times together. Sometimes we were joined by Ernest Morton, another white boy, and Lee Brown, a coloured boy, but George and I were especially friendly. Many a day he would sit at the table with the family and I would be keeping the flies off and waiting on the table, when we would wink at each other and make plans as to what we would do when dinner was over and my other work done. Often he would pitch in and help me through and then off we went fishing on Sailor Creek, famous for one of the skirmishes between Lee and Grant, on the way to Appomattox after the evacuation of Richmond.

We not only enjoyed our boyish play, but we worked many examples in arithmetic together and discussed history as well. I remember that we differed frequently. One of the discussions we used to have most often was about which was the greater general, Grant or Lee. He was for Lee; I for Grant. We often discussed the merits of the conflict between the states, which culminated in the war. I could never swerve him from his position on this question and he never swerved me from mine. We never found it profitable to discuss this issue. He would sometimes lose his temper, and I frequently lost mine. There came a time when we ceased to discuss it entirely and I think our relations were consequently very much the more pleasant. He had a most excellent father, and the son was of the same type —very bright, always frank, always generous—and he never swerved in his friendship for me.

I sometimes feared that the Vaughan's and the Reverend Mr. Denney, George's father, were a little annoyed that he preferred apparently to be out in the fields where I was with the cows and sheep, or even to help me

*A light two-wheeled vehicle having a seat for the driver only.

with my chores, to being in the house among the guests—for the Vaughan household was a very popular meeting place for young people and old. It was a great social centre and the scene of many parties.

Mr. Vaughan's death, which occurred about this time, made everything different at "Pleasant Shade" thereafter. The farm was divided among the children. Most of the coloured people moved away. My father went to live with a family of Mortons who were by marriage connected with the Vaughan family. Mr. J.X. Morton, who afterward became a professor at the Virginia Polytechnic Institute, had a son Ernest, to whom I have referred. Our friendship grew stronger; indeed he left parents and everything else to be with my coloured chum Lee and with me, and we, in the same spirit, neglected everything that we could with impunity, in order that the three of us could be together. We fished and hunted together and engaged in many boyish sports and pranks. Nothing in his possession was too good for us, and nothing in ours was too good for him. As we grew older my father did not wholly approve of this intimacy, and used often to say that we were "too thick to thrive." In the course of time, there did come a parting. Ernest went off to school and my chum Lee and I were left on his father's farm. The weeks immediately following his leaving for the Virginia Polytechnic Institute were dull and dreary for us at home. This I think was in October. I continued to work on the farm, for I was now too big for chores, and went to school when the weather did not permit working on the farm. I was anxiously awaiting the Christmas holidays when our friend Ernest would return and we would again have some good times together. He would tell us no doubt of his college experiences and we had some experiences that we could relate to him. At last the day came. Lee and I were at the house when they brought him in the carriage from Rice's Depot. His father and one of his sisters had gone to meet him. He had with him also his roommate, I think, who had come to spend the holidays with him. They both wore gray uniforms with brass buttons. Lee and I, as soon as Ernest alighted from the carriage, rushed up to shake hands. He not only did not shake hands with us but his manner was as cold and frigid as the north wind that we were breathing. He did bow, but it was quickly done. Lee went home. I went into the kitchen with Aunt Viny, the cook. I was feeling bad; so was Lee. I was thinking. Sometimes I wonder if I ever thought quite as seriously on life as I did that night. A few moments later he came out into the kitchen in his splendid spick and span uniform with brass buttons and polished shoes. Aunt Viny, the old cook of sixty or seventy years, rushed up to him and threw her arms around him, exclaiming, "My chil'! My chil'!" and he in turn threw his arms around her. He was not more demonstrative toward his mother; in fact, not even so much so, because his mother was not so demonstrative as the cook. I sat unhappy, puzzled, thinking. Finally, through the darkness of the night, I stole down through the ravine, across the brook, and up to our cabin on the hill. I went to bed early that night. My father, who always saw and realized much more than he ever expressed, asked me the one question that I did not care to have him ask, and he made just the one ejaculation which cut keen and deep. He said, "Did you see Ernest?" "Yes, Sir," I said. "What did he say to you?" "Nothing," said I. "I told you to stay away from there," he said. I made no answer. He said no more. He knew how I felt, for he probably imagined what had happened. I went immediately to bed, as I have said, earlier than was my custom, and I think remained in bed later next morning, but I slept less than usual. I was thinking that night.

I arose next morning more weary than when I went to bed; but I was wiser and more resolute than ever before in my life. I went through my usual day's work on the farm and looked after the hogs for the Mortons, and did what I had to do with reference to the feeding, but did not go to the house except as I was obliged to do. I met Ernest and his chum face to face. I looked the other way. I do not think they noticed where I was looking. I am sure they did not care. I was trying to snub them both. It had no effect, so far as I could judge, on either. But before going to bed the following night I had firmly resolved that getting an education was the best thing toward which I could bend my efforts in the future.

The next morning I asked my father about the school for coloured people, which was being projected under the influence of General Mahone at Petersburg, now a State Normal School. He told me much about it. It was to open the following fall. The Hon. John M. Langston, he said, a coloured man who was as well educated as any white person that he knew of, was to be the president. He said I might go if I wished and that he would do what he could to help me. It being a state school, and he having certain strong friends in the Republican Party (General Mahone among them), Hon. B.S. Hooper, a member of Congress from the Fourth Congressional District of Virginia, would probably arrange for me to have a scholarship. He also told me much about Hampton Institute but he was not enthusiastic about my going to Hampton. He said Hampton was a "work school" and that he could teach me as much about work as Hampton could; but as he thought I could go to Hampton without any money, he would permit me to go if I insisted, though it was against his inclinations.

During the winter I did much thinking, and much talking, too, with those people whose judgment I thought I could trust, about going to school, either at Hampton or at Petersburg. Mention was also made of some other schools. Captain Frank Southall, whose brother, Dr. J.W. Southall, was later Superintendent of Public Instruction of Virginia, learned through some source that I contemplated going to school. He had somehow been impressed with my knowledge of the Bible and my interest in the Sunday School by my attendance at the afternoon Sunday School at the Jamestown Presbyterian Church, to which I have referred, and of which he was superintendent. He wanted me to go to a school at Tuscaloosa, Alabama, to fit myself for the ministry in the Presbyterian Church. He said he would gladly arrange this and that the entire expense would be provided. This did not appeal to me very much, because I was unwilling to sign an agreement that I would enter the ministry or join the Presbyterian Church. All of my people were Baptists and we were living in a strongly Baptist community, that is, so far as Negroes were concerned. The Negroes, at least in my community at that time, looked with more or less suspicion upon the religion of white people anyway, and the feeling between denominations was strong; so, while I was determined to get an education, I replied that I preferred to be an ignorant Baptist rather than an educated Presbyterian. In my youthful zeal I told others of the offer I had had from Captain Southall and of my determination to keep the faith, repeating the expression that I preferred being an ignorant Baptist rather than an educated Presbyterian, and this expression never failed to bring forth much approval and applause from the coloured people of the community.

Chapter 3

Through Reconstruction

THE following spring I joined a party of young men and secured work in Surry County in a lumber camp near the James River. My hope was to save sufficient money to pay my way through school. I had talked very frankly with my friends regarding schools, and had about decided that I would enter the school at Petersburg. I worked in this camp about two years, and succeeded in making my way up successively from piling lumber, through the grade of an experienced tree chopper—which meant that I had a pretty thorough knowledge of the quality of lumber in a tree before it was cut down, knowing by certain definite signs evident to a lumberman whether a tree was sound or decayed—to the post of foreman of a squad, having in charge the sorting and grading of lumber.

One is apt to think of seventy five or more lumbermen as a rough, lawless, and undesirable group, fitted only for the heavy work connected with lumbering. As a matter of fact, there were a few rough men, who, in every sense, lived up to that reputation, but in the Ferguson camp there was a large number of honest, hard working, thrifty men who came mostly from Prince Edward, Amelia, and Dinwiddie counties in Virginia. Many of them were ambitious for schooling. Some few had had some experience in politics and therefore kept posted on what was going on in Virginia.

The "Readjuster Movement" had just been introduced. This had caused the fusion of many Republicans and Democrats into what was known as the Readjuster Party. We had little or nothing to do with the people native to Surry County; the truth of the matter was, they didn't permit us to, because of our reputation. A few of us went to Sunday School and attended church services at Cypress Baptist Church, five miles away, and got somewhat into the social life of the coloured community. Beyond this a number of the men, in order to spend their leisure time profitably, organized a debating club, holding at intervals a mock court or a mock assembly, copying as nearly as we could the Virginia Legislature. Almost every night in the week there was something going on in connection with some one of these organizations.

I remember one man from Dinwiddie County, George Edwards, who had for many years served as magistrate in his precinct. He was reasonably well educated and had been a school teacher. He was well versed in politics and everything else that had to do with public affairs in Virginia. He it was who guided us for the most part in these activities. There were others almost as well trained. I think I have never had any experience I enjoyed any more than the winter nights in that camp; and I got from this experience a certain sort of training that I have since in many ways found very useful. I got also a taste for politics and other civic affairs that might have changed my career but for certain conscientious scruples of my mother's.

I recall also how shocked we were at the tidings that President Garfield had been shot. When we later learned of his death, we thought it proper to suspend all public activities in the camp for a week as a mark of respect to the President.

Evening meetings, especially on Saturdays, brought out sometimes large numbers of local people, white and coloured; and the manager of the camp became so well pleased with the effect that he gave us Saturday afternoon once a month, and invited many people from surrounding communities as well as from other saw-mills — and there were many saw-mills in the neighbourhood — to witness these monthly public exercises.

During the two years that I spent in that camp in Surry County, I saved comparatively little money; but I got something from the work itself, and the intimate contact with this group of men — the debating societies, the glee club, the prayer meetings, and other activities — which has had a very strong influence upon my later life.

An attack of malaria fever made it necessary for me to leave this marshy section on the James River. At the doctor's suggestion I returned to my home in Prince Edward County. My return home was in the late summer of 1882 and I found the political atmosphere very "thick and heavy." I was asked frequently to speak at political mass meetings, and I pitched in with vigour, taking up the cudgels for the "Readjuster Movement," about which, however, I knew little. This was a movement on the part of the Fusion Party for the readjustment of the state debt. All Negroes had a vote in those days. Negro Democrats were very few, only about a half dozen or so being found in a county. I remember the impression created on the mass of coloured people — and white people, too, for that matter — when I appeared at a picnic in the Vaughan woods and made a surprisingly effective political speech. I knew little about the subject, and was as much surprised as any one at the impression made and the enthusiasm over my speech displayed by the large number of people present. But the impression was so strong that when the meeting was over I was taken aside by three or four white men and as many coloured, who decided then and there that I should have the nomination for the Lower House of the State Legislature from my district. They decided what the ticket should be; that there should be certain white men and myself as the one coloured man. I was especially urged to this step by Walker Blanton, a shrewd, keen, coloured man, who did not know one letter of the alphabet from the other, but who was nevertheless the political leader of the district among the coloured people and withal a very useful citizen. I was inclined to accept the proposition, but there were one or two strong obstacles in the way. One was that I had planned to go to school, but the really serious one was that I was not yet twenty one years of age. The white people in the group said that they could arrange the age situation, that nobody could prove exactly when I was born, and that I was large and mature in appearance, so that question would hardly arise in any case; and one gentleman in the group said that he knew my mother and father and the whole family connection and, moreover, had the family Bible record of all of them, so that he could easily adjust them in a way that would stand any test. The coloured men were equally zealous, making their plea on the ground that I had more education than any coloured man in the precinct, which was enough; that I could at least read and write and figure, and that was not true in Virginia of all the legislators even. The temptation was very great. I had just about decided to accept. Everything was to be arranged by the leaders of the Readjuster Party in the county. The only thing then left would be the formal notification a few weeks afterward. But my mother when approached said that she could not raise my age, and would be unwilling to swear to anything but the truth; that she knew exactly the day and year and hour of my birth. My father was non committal. He felt that my mother was too conscientious and that there were lots of probabilities of her being mistaken, and, too, that she would be perfectly safe in saying she was not absolutely sure and leaving it to the white people to settle the rest. But my mother stood firm, so the committee, finding that they could not get her to agree to sign the affidavit, concluded that the matter was at an end. Another coloured man was nominated and later elected. I confess I was somewhat relieved and not very sorry that my mother had taken such a firm stand. To be sure there was some disappointment, but I am confident that I slept better as a result of my mother's decision.

About this time a young man by the name of Edward D. Stewart, a graduate of Hampton Institute, came to teach in the school in our district which I had attended at intervals for some years. I was able to get from him first hand information about Hampton. He gave me facts regarding the inner working of the school: how a student could enter, the kind of work he would do, the studies he would have, and something of what the men accomplished after graduating. He felt sure that I would have no difficulty in entering and in completing the course of studies. He thought my greatest difficulty would be in overcoming the popularity which I had achieved in my home community. He suggested that I would have to put all that behind me and assume that I did not know so much as I thought I did or as others in my community thought I did. He feared it would be difficult for me to adapt myself to the discipline of the school at Hampton. I was at this time leader of the church choir, superintendent of the Sunday School, and might have been a deacon, but was considered too young for that particular place. In some ways I was considered a very important man in what was then a rather backward community.

I wrote to General Armstrong, the principal of Hampton, my letter being endorsed by Mr. Stewart. General Armstrong gave me an immediate reply in his own handwriting, saying that I might come to Hampton and work in the knitting room. Mr. Stewart advised that I had better wait until I could get work on the farm at Shellbanks or at the saw-mill. He knew something of my knowledge of lumber and experience in farming, stock raising, and similar lines. He advised against my learning to knit mittens or working in the house under any circumstances. He had the feeling that knitting room boys at Hampton did not succeed very well, for some fell into bad ways, a good many were disciplined severely, and a few suspended. So, at his suggestion, I wrote asking that I might have a place either on the farm or at the saw-mill, which work, I considered, was better adapted to my size and strength. Not long afterward I received a letter to the effect that I might come and that they would find satisfactory work for a boy who showed such good sense in his choice of occupation.

I took my departure on Sunday morning from the cabin where we were then living. The night before I was given a "party." It would be called a "reception" now. To be sure, it was in a log cabin and there were a great many people present. The young folk indulged in games of various kinds but the older ones, the church members especially, took the whole matter more seriously. I recall that just before we parted there were many speeches. They were all crude, as I think of it now, yet I have seldom witnessed a more sincere and touching farewell reception. Our old pastor, Armstead Berkeley, who was perhaps seventy six years of age, officiated as master of ceremonies. He had a wonderfully fine voice, strong and melodious. He was a great singer and had all the qualities necessary to make him a fervid, emotional speaker. I have known him at revival meetings to offer prayer, and again and again I have seen educated white people present who could scarcely control their features for the tears which ran down their cheeks. He made the final speech and closed the affair with a very earnest and touching prayer; and while there had been much levity among the young folk the early part of the night, he left them all in a very serious mood. I could not respond when called upon, but the impression of the sincere affection and good will of those simple, earnest people with whom I had lived from childhood has always remained with me.

My old chum, Lee Brown, and a few friends took my little trunk on a mule cart next morning, and we drove about five miles to Rice's Depot where I took the train for Norfolk, Virginia. Here I transferred to the Baltimore steamer which ordinarily touched at Old Point about seven o'clock at night. It so happened that because of a very severe storm the captain of the steamer decided that he would not touch at Old Point, so I was carried on with many other passengers to Baltimore. This was entirely against my wishes and naturally I was much annoyed. The ship's crew were very kind to all of us and gave us our meals and made no additional charge for the extra trip. This being my first experience on a steamboat, I suffered the discomforts that are common to the average passenger sailing on a stormy night. I spent a most interesting day in Baltimore strolling around, but did not get very far from the wharf.

Chapter 4

Doing and Learning

THAT night I took the same steamer on which I had arrived and landed at Old Point the following morning, the 13th of October, 1885. I took a hack, which carried me and my little trunk past Fortress Monroe and up through the little town of Phoebus, then Mill Creek, and on to the grounds of the Hampton Institute. It was to me the most beautiful place I had ever seen. We drove up through the school farm past the old Butler School. This was a school that had been built under the direction of General Butler during the Civil War for the children of the freedmen, out of the lumber that had been used, much of it, in hospital barracks. We passed on through many acres of vegetables which Hampton had cultivated, and past the National Soldiers' Home cemetery, where stood some four thousand or more marble headstones, marking the final resting place of men who gave their all to preserve the Union. It is interesting that in that same cemetery, cared for by the Federal Government, there are many hundreds of Confederate soldiers also. Looking upon the well kept grounds of the Institute, the water front, the neat and imposing buildings and farm lands, I felt almost as if I were in another world. A few mischievous boys took occasion to have some fun at my expense. They were already calling out "fresh fish," and two or three of them yanked my small trunk out of the carriage and balanced it on their fingers as waiters balance their trays in hotels. Some suggested that it weighed ten pounds; others, five. One little fellow, by the name of Bates, as I remember, whom I afterward found to be a fine baseball player, wanted to bet it would weigh not over two and three fourths pounds. I must confess that the small trunk was entirely out of proportion to the size of its 175 pound, eighteen year old, and somewhat awkward, owner. But I went through the ordeal good naturedly, and finally one of the older boys was kind enough to show me to the office where I presented myself to the commandant, the Rev. George L. Curtis, who later served for many years as a clergyman in Bloomfield, N.J. He sent me for examination to Miss

Anna G. Baldwin, the head teacher in the night school. She seemed to me very cold and unsympathetic, but I found afterward that I had misjudged her. She was, in fact, kind and very sympathetic; though her manner, like that of many New Englanders, was cold, austere, and very businesslike. The white women with whom I had dealt before had in their manner and speech a certain sympathetic quality that put one rather at ease than otherwise. Anyhow, I failed utterly to pass the entrance examination, though it seemed even at that time to be easy. I think I was bewildered. Everything was new and confusing. Baltimore experiences, my sea sickness, so many students, the battalion and band—all were so strange that I found it difficult even to see the print which was given me to read or the figures with which I was working. I was very much upset over my failure. I returned to the office and handed Mr. Curtis the note which announced it. He, too, seemed very much disappointed. He was at the same time sympathetic and told me frankly that he was very sorry that I had not passed. From what I had told him of the work I had done in school he had thought I would have no difficulty in passing, but would make a rather high class. He passed the note to Mr. F.C. Briggs, then the business agent of Hampton Institute, who sat at a desk near him. The two whispered some words, to which, at the time, I did not think it improper for me to listen. Mr. Briggs remarked— and, by the way, I thought all the time Mr. Briggs was General Armstrong —in an undertone to Mr. Curtis, "It is too bad. I like his face. He has a very honest look," adding, "I think you had better keep him if you can." Mr. Curtis then turned to me with the words, "Well, young man, what are you going to do? You have failed to pass your examination to enter even the lowest class." I told him that I had come to stay at any cost, and that I thought my failure was due to my new surroundings; that I had not been in school for about two years, but had read an occasional newspaper and an occasional book when I could get hold of one, but had done no work in arithmetic except of the simplest kind and had written only an occasional letter, so that I thought I was "rusty." He wanted to know if I had any objection to hard work. I assured him I was not afraid of hard work, that I had worked hard all my life; so he said he would give me a choice of work, asking whether I would like to go to the kitchen or to the farm or whether I would prefer the saw-mill. As I had worked at a saw-mill and had some knowledge of lumber, I preferred the saw-mill, and was so assigned. I found this mill much larger and much more complicated than any I had seen before. I was put under the charge of a student, Edward R. Jackson, whom the boys called "Big Jack." He was to instruct me in Hampton's methods of grading and piling lumber. I was also admitted on trial to the lowest class in the night school.

On the second afternoon of my saw-mill work, while piling lumber with Big Jack, the Rev. H. B. Frissell, the school chaplain and vice principal, came up and engaged us, or rather me, in conversation. He knew Jackson, for Jackson was then in what was known as the Pastor's Class, the School for Bible Study at Hampton, where he was then fitting himself for the ministry. He afterward became a minister and had a large church in Alexandria, Virginia, where for many years he did very effective work as a teacher and preacher.

Mr. Frissell asked me many questions: if I was happy at Hampton; whether I liked the place and people. He inquired about my home and family. His kindly expressed wish that I should have a successful career at Hampton, and his assurance that I was in the midst of friends made a deep impression on me, and strengthened very much my determination to remain at Hampton and to succeed, for that afternoon I had been experiencing a certain kind of longing for home that affected me more than at any time during my entire stay at the Institute. Later I was transferred from piling lumber to a raft of logs in the creek to get off the chains. I was shown how to perform this operation by another Virginia boy by the name of John H. Palmer. He went about his work very quietly and always most faithfully and steadily, and as he showed me how to remove the chains I was impressed by his kindness and patience. It is more than interesting that this same J. H. Palmer is now registrar at Tuskegee Institute, where for many years he has been just as kind and faithful as an officer as on that day thirty-four years ago when he showed me how to take the chains off of logs that were brought from North Carolina, through the Dismal Swamp, across Hampton Roads to the school saw-mill.

I remember so well my first Sunday night at Hampton. Six hundred or more students — Negroes and Indians — with a hundred or more white people, assembled for evening prayers. A modest, unassuming gentleman, with a soothing voice, conducted the services. I do not remember the passage he read, but there were two or three petitions in his prayer that stirred my youthful emotions and brought over me a feeling hard then and hard now to describe. A few days before, amid unattractive, meagre cabin surroundings, I had bidden good-bye to an earnest, hard-working, devoted, Christian mother. In this simple yet inspiring prayer, Mr. Frissell, who had so kindly spoken to me a few days before, asked God's blessing upon the humble mothers and fathers in all of the homes represented by the young people before him, the poorest as well as the best; and he prayed that, amid the pleasant surroundings of Hampton Institute, the young people would always remember their parents who did not live, all of them, in such an environment as we had at Hampton. It seemed most strange to me, amid new surroundings and so many new faces, that everybody should turn aside from work and study, and that this gentleman, a stranger to me, should be thinking, as I supposed, about my old mother, and that he should put in such beautiful words the very thoughts and feelings which were in my own mind. From that night I made up my mind that Hampton was a very good place for me to be, and from that night also I knew Mr. Frissell was our friend, that he was interested in all that concerned us, that he was a man in whom I could confide.

The students sang plantation songs, the religious folk songs of the Negro. I had been brought up on this kind of music and was very familiar with many of the songs that were sung, but somehow there was something about this singing—led by a tall, very handsome black man with a deep and melodious baritone voice—with the four parts blending almost as if there were just one great voice singing, that almost carried me into a new world. I had never heard such singing, but somehow, notwithstanding my thorough enjoyment of the music, the dress, and manner of the pupils, and my real appreciation of being in such a wonderful institution, I was disappointed to hear these songs sung by educated people and in an educational institution. I had expected to hear regular church music such as would be sung by white people mostly, and such as was written as I supposed by white people also. I had come to school to learn to do things differently; to sing, to speak, and to use the language, and of course, the music, not of coloured people but of white people.

One of my newly made friends, Thomas B. Patterson, who sat next me in chapel, and with whom I worked at the saw-mill, and who to this day is noted for his frankness of expression, whispered to me, saying, "What do you think of that music?" My reply was, "The singing is all right but this is no place for it." As the group of us walked on toward our quarters I did not hesitate to express my opinion regarding this music and most of the new boys agreed emphatically with my attitude. One or two of the older students argued that the songs were beautiful and people enjoyed them so why should we not sing them. The only reply I could give was that they were Negro songs and that we had come to Hampton to learn something better; and then, too, I objected to exhibiting the religious and emotional side of our people to white folks; for I supposed the latter listened to these songs simply for entertainment and perhaps amusement. I had frequently seen white people at Negro gatherings in my own community, and had the feeling that many of them came merely to be entertained. I remember how strongly I felt many years before then when I attended Robinson's circus in our little village of Farmville. I remember the animals, of which I had only seen pictures before, and also the ring performances—fancy riding, antics of the clowns, and so forth. At the close of the main performance a concert was announced and my last ten cents was paid for it. Some twenty or thirty men with faces blackened appeared in a semicircle with banjos, tambourines, and the like. The stories they told and the performances they gave were indeed most interesting to me, but I remember how shocked I was when they sang, "Wear dem Golden Slippers to Walk dem Golden Streets," two men dancing to the tune exactly as it was sung by the people in the Negro churches of my community. This song was as sacred to me as "Nearer, My God, to Thee" or "Old Hundred." I felt that these white men were making fun, not only of our colour and of our songs, but also of our religion. It took three years of training at Hampton Institute to bring me to the point of being willing to sing Negro songs in the presence of white people. White minstrels with black faces have done more than any other single agency to lower the tone of Negro music and cause the Negro to despise his own songs. Indeed, the feeling of the average Negro today is that the average white man expects him to "jump jim-crow" or do the buffoon act, whether in music or in other things. It is a source of gratification, therefore, to Negroes generally that Fisk University, Hampton Institute, Tuskegee Institute, with many other Negro educational institutions, have persistently preserved and used the folk music of their people, in keeping with the spirit of its origin, thus not only elevating it in the estimation of coloured people, but causing others also to appreciate its value and beauty.

A few Sunday evenings later, when General Armstrong had returned to the Institute, he spoke in his own forceful manner to the students about respecting themselves, their race, their history, their traditions, their songs, and folk lore in general. He referred then to the Negro songs as "a priceless legacy," which he hoped every Negro student would always cherish. I was impressed with him and with his address, but I was not entirely convinced.

However, I was led to think along a little different line regarding my race. The truth is it was the first time I had ever given any serious thought to anything distinctively Negro. This also was the first time in my life that I had begun to think that there was anything that the Negro had that was deserving of particular consideration. This meant a readjustment of values that was not particularly easy for a raw country lad.

I think it was in December of 1885 or late in November that a group of boys, of which I was one, was returning from the Soldiers' home, which is separated from Hampton Institute only by a creek. We had noticed, before going over, a coloured man going through the engine room and boiler room and over the lumber yard looking at the machinery, lumber, saw-mill, planing-mill, etc., And we met this same man on our return going through the orchard, the farm, and the truck garden. We wondered who this man could be who seemed rather familiar with things at Hampton, and at the same time appeared to be very much interested in all the work of the place. When we went to chapel that night this gentleman sat next to General Armstrong on the platform in the old Whitin chapel. There were many visitors from the hotels and the town as well as the regular audience, and there were more teachers in chapel than usual. It was the first time I had seen a coloured man on the speaker's platform. We were glad, and took much pride, as the Negro students generally did, in any honour that came to a coloured man at Hampton; that is, any special recognition that came from General Armstrong.

After the usual devotional exercises General Armstrong, in his characteristic way, introduced this gentleman to the audience. He presented him as Booker T. Washington of Tuskegee. I remember now what a beautiful introduction General Armstrong gave him. He spoke of the possibilities of the work at Tuskegee and felt very sure that Tuskegee would some day be as large as Hampton, if not larger, and he predicted that Booker T. Washington would eventually be recognized as one of America's most distinguished citizens. He made this statement, he said, because he was thoroughly acquainted with the man of whom he was speaking. Booker Washington, he said, had been one of his boys; that he had served as his private secretary, and that he had recommended him for the work in Alabama. That during the past five years he had had wonderful success in gaining the good will of the white people and the coloured people surrounding the Institute and that the North had responded to his appeals for aid. Indeed General Armstrong had given no one so strong and, it seemed to us, so flattering an introduction, though many distinguished visitors had already appeared on that platform since I had entered school. There was not much known then of Booker T. Washington, though General Armstrong and others had frequently referred to him and the work which he had started at Tuskegee in Alabama. Even at this time General Armstrong had pointed him out as a sample of what he hoped the Hampton students would look forward to becoming after completing their education. He hoped they would start schools on the Hampton plan in rural communities.

While we were pleased at the introduction, we were anxious that this coloured man should measure up with his address to what General Armstrong said in the presence of so many white people, to say nothing of the coloured people. It made us all the more anxious that the coloured man should appear to good advantage, and I confess, as I think of it now, the appearance of the speaker did not impress us strongly. I remember some boys whispered, "We're gone tonight."

There is something pathetic sometimes, I think, about the anxiety on the part of coloured people that one of their number shall show up to good advantage. The conditions under which we live, the early predictions that the Negro would not succeed, and the persistent comment that he is an inferior individual, have created in the race an anxiety and an earnest desire that every effort the Negro puts forth shall be of the best. We were especially anxious, therefore, that on that occasion he should "hit the bull's-eye," as we used to say. He had not spoken many minutes before all of our anxiety had disappeared. He started off by telling a story which I do not recall at this time, but I know it was something about eating partridges. He spoke of what he was trying to do at Tuskegee Institute and said, modestly, that he was trying to carry out, as any graduate should do, the ideas of General Armstrong and Hampton. He spoke clearly of the importance and value of trade education and pointed out the fact that the men who had learned their trades in slavery were passing and that white men were taking their places. He emphasized the importance of rural life, buying farms, good homes, and the degradation of one-room-cabin life, and while he did not in any way belittle college education, he did emphasize the fundamental need of trade education, the buying of land, the building of homes, bank accounts, etc. These, he declared, were essential to the highest development of any people.

As I think of it now, and as I thought of it then, we considered it perhaps the most remarkable address we had ever heard, and coming from a coloured man, about whom we had felt so much anxiety, it was all the more impressive. We were not expected to applaud in chapel at Sunday evening services, but there was a spontaneous outburst of applause from the audience when he sat down, and it was prolonged. General Armstrong arose, remarking, "I am glad you had the good sense to break the rule on such an occasion." He added, "This is for me as well as for you a very happy hour." It is unnecessary to remark that that address was the talk of the year among the students and teachers. We had some Indian friends who used to come to our rooms after meetings of this sort. I recall now that until "taps", some eight or ten of us, with our Indian friends, discussed that speech. One of the latter, John Archambeau, remarked to the group that the only fault he found with Booker Washington was the fact that he was not an Indian.

My twelve months' work at the saw-mill was hard and difficult, but we got out of it a great deal of pleasure and satisfaction. I, with my associates, learned a great many things, especially about lumber and machinery. I learned among other things to fire a huge boiler, something of the quality of coal, and how to get the most out of it. I learned to run the big Corliss engine, much about steam fitting, and a good deal about carpentry work, though I had worked for awhile as a carpenter before.

There were about twenty-two boys who worked at the saw-mill with me during that year. The record of those boys since leaving Hampton—what they have done—would be interesting reading. Mr. William T. Westwood, our foreman, an ex Confederate soldier, had very high ideals and insisted, frequently against our private protests, that we live up to his standards of work and neatness in piling lumber, as well as in our personal appearance in overalls. Even to this day, though no longer connected with the school, he continues to take a very personal interest in all of the young men who come under his instruction.

I closed my year at the saw-mill in October, 1886, when I entered the regular day school. During the previous year I had worked in the day and attended school at night. This was customary among students who did not have the means to enter the day school directly. I had the choice between entering the highest class in the Junior Grade or the lowest class in the Middle Year; for I had been promoted from the lowest class in night school after three months, and was already a Junior in regular standing in the school. Inasmuch as I would be entering the higher class with two conditions and the lower class with no conditions, I preferred the highest Junior Grade to the lowest Middle, much to the satisfaction of the head teacher,

Miss Mary F. Mackie, to whom Doctor Washington referred in "Up From Slavery" as the one who gave him that now-famous entrance examination. But I knew my weakness and I knew my deficiencies in English particularly, one of the subjects in which I would have been conditioned; and I knew further that if I missed the Junior training, I would probably be handicapped for the remainder of my course. It was also true that my knowledge of geography was rather limited—I would have been conditioned in that also—so I made my choice advisedly.

Soon after this I was made an officer in the battalion and was given charge of one of the boys' buildings, being responsible to the commandant for the physical care of the building as well as for the conduct of its occupants. I recalled that my father yielded under protest to my coming to Hampton as a work student, urging me to wait another year while he and I saved sufficient money so that I could go to Petersburg and not be obliged to do work in the school. He felt, and I shared his feeling to some extent, that I knew all there was to know about work, but somehow I discovered during my year as a work student that I was constantly running against new things and new ways of doing old things: in the care of my own room, in the drill, at the saw-mill, in the night school; and even in the dining room and on the playground my vision grew continually wider and larger and I became more skilled in many ways with many and various things. That work year was a sort of initiation into an entirely new life, new surroundings, new people, different races, new standards, new ideas and ideals; and I have always been glad that, in spite of my father's protest, I had come not because I wished to work, but rather because I did not wish to delay another year in getting an education—and had taken this year of work at Hampton Institute. But the first year in day school was different. I assimilated, perhaps unconsciously, many of these new ideals. While I learned many valuable lessons from books during this first year, they were insignificant as compared with the indescribable something which I gathered outside of books, very real at Hampton, and very real to me, too, which I cannot accurately describe in writing, but which was nevertheless very pronounced and very definite.

In my next year, I came in daily contact with a half dozen or more lady teachers of the sturdy, to austere, exacting, yet very kindly New England type; and while many of the subjects which they taught were not entirely new, the presentation was so different and they brought in so many practical, daily-life problems, not put down in books, that I found myself for the first few months in a realm almost as strange and different as my first year. One of the most striking subjects, as I think of it, was natural history or zoölogy, which was taught by Miss Ford, who afterward became the wife of General Armstrong. Our collection of numerous specimens, the investigation and dissecting of various insects and animals, the use of the microscope, were all a constant revelation to me of my dense ignorance concerning the common, every-day things with which I had been dealing and about which I had thought I knew so much. Mrs. Armstrong was a wonderfully strong teacher, able to arouse tremendous enthusiasm among her pupils, not only to master what was in the textbook, but also to augment this by their own investigation and research in order to test the accuracy of the textbook. I think also that my work in mathematics under Miss J. E. Davis, a graduate of Vassar College; in geography, under Miss Mary E. Coates; in grammar, under Miss M. J. Sherman, a graduate of Wellesley College, together with my work under others made for me a most interesting, inspiring, and helpful year.

I recall, too, as I am sure every Hampton student does who came under their instruction and care, the helpfulness of Miss Helen W. Ludlow and her intimate friend, Dr. Martha M. Waldron, the resident physician of the Institute, in many other things besides books and studies. Their loyalty to General Armstrong, and their devotion to Hampton through many years of service, had much to do with making the life and work of Hampton possible. I was not surprised at the end of the year, when the announcement was made of my name with many others for promotion to the Middle Class. I was so much impressed with the life at Hampton, and had enjoyed so much the use of the library, where there were more books than I had ever seen before in one place (to all of which I had free access, as had all students) that I asked if I might remain there for the summer vacation and be given work, the money that had been placed to my credit during my work year having been considerably reduced. I thought that perhaps by remaining I would not only save more money through having less opportunity to spend, but that I would also have the use of the library and be in the atmosphere of educated people, which was much to my liking. I was accordingly assigned to work for the summer, and was given more responsibility In connection with the battalion as well as with the young men generally. It proved a very pleasant and very profitable summer. I went home for a vacation of two weeks in August—my first trip away from the school since I had entered nearly two years before. I was very anxious to see my parents and friends, and, of course, was equally anxious, I think, to show my uniform with my first lieutenant's shoulder straps. Everyone was glad to see me, white as well as coloured, and the older white people were especially cordial. One thing I noticed which I could not at that time explain was that many of the young white men with whom I had grown up were much less cordial than their parents, and frequently they avoided me and only greeted me after I had greeted them.

I attended the church and the Sunday School and I think I never had a more cordial welcome anywhere, with more consideration, or one giving me more real pleasure, than that from these people at Macedonia Baptist Church, with which I had been connected in one way or another since its organization. And certainly no mother ever had any more real pride in her son and his appearance than mine at that time. It was hard for me to get out of her sight. She insisted on going with me almost everywhere I went.

Returning from Macedonia Church with my mother the first Sunday after my return, we were pleasantly surprised to meet Mr. William L. Vaughan and his wife as they were driving home from the Jamestown Presbyterian Church. Seeing me with my mother they stopped and greeted us very cordially. I was very glad to see them and apparently they were equally glad to see me. Before parting they asked me to come over and spend the day with them, which I did on the following Tuesday, when they sent their carriage and driver to my mother's home to take me over. Mr. Vaughan devoted the entire day to me, taking me over the farm on horseback, looking at the stock, acres of tobacco and corn, and showing me other points of interest about the place. He also asked many questions about Hampton Institute and about my courses of study and progress there, showing a deep interest in all that I was doing, as well as in my future. He expressed much satisfaction in the fact that I had gone to school rather than into politics and possibly into the Legislature, for he knew of the incident in my experience a few years before, to which I have already referred.

Of course I was greatly interested in all that he showed me on his splendid farm, but I was more impressed with the attention and courtesy which he accorded me during the day. And I did not fail to notice that he gave me the same consideration in many ways that he and his father had bestowed upon their guests of former years when I worked as a boy upon their plantation. While I very much enjoyed the two weeks at home visiting old scenes and old friends, there was nevertheless an clear element of sadness in it all. The dwellings, barns, and fences were unkempt; there was an air of disorder and confusion about most things and most people also; our church and the choir, as well as the sermon of our pastor, seemed so different and disappointing and so unsatisfactory that I was rather relieved to get away from it. Before leaving I discussed this with my mother; but she felt that things were not so very different, that many things were actually better, that the difference was with me. I had changed. I have no doubt she was correct, as she usually was.

I returned to Hampton after an interesting and pleasant, though in some ways disappointing, visit, but I was never before so impressed with the needs of my community along almost every line. I was convinced that whatever else I might do, there was nothing more worth while than helping just such people in just that kind of a community.

Chapter 5

A Touch of Real Life

THE Middle Year at Hampton was not very different from the Junior. The one subject which I think had the greatest influence on me was the theory and practice of teaching. They rarely called it "pedagogy" in those days. I think that at Hampton they were afraid to use such a "big" word. As a part of Hampton's course in practice teaching every student, before entering the Senior Class, was required to teach at least one term or its equivalent in the public schools. It was for this reason that the course in pedagogics was taken up in the Middle Year, and a certificate given by Hampton to its Senior students to teach in the schools of Virginia; but most superintendents required that every applicant should pass his examination. I enjoyed the work in practice teaching very much. I do not know that it was the subject that impressed me so much as did the teacher, Miss Elizabeth Hyde, who conducted the class, and who has ever since been one of the strongest and most helpful forces in the life and work of Hampton Institute. We had at least a part of the time of nearly every recitation taken up in a sort of conference on human nature. We did not call it psychology then, but that is what it was, and even to this day I am influenced by many of the conclusions that we then reached.

At the close of the year, with seventy-eight other students, I was passed on to the Senior Class and was provided with a certificate to teach in the schools of Virginia, provided, of course, that I could pass the county examination satisfactorily. It occurred to me that, before teaching, inasmuch as I had never been outside of Virginia except on my enforced visit to Baltimore, it would strengthen my position in my school community, wherever it might be, if I could at least say that I had lived outside of Virginia; so I secured a position as head waiter in a hotel in Pennsylvania. I had what the boys would call in those days "a very successful season." While my work was not very hard from some points of view and my pay was very generous, at least in gratuities—"tips"—there was something about the life that did not appeal to me, because the conduct of some of the guests differed greatly from what I had expected. So far as the treatment received from the guests was concerned, I had no cause for complaint, but many things about them and their manner of living were disappointing, not to say shocking, to one who had set up a very high standard and rather high ideals for people of means and education who lived amidst such pleasant and apparently wholesome surroundings.

At the close of the summer season I returned to Virginia and was appointed to teach in the school at Cottontown in Cumberland County. I had taken the examination in Prince Edward County, for this was the county in which I lived, but inasmuch as all the places in the schools in that county were filled I was recommended to the superintendent of Cumberland County. I had no serious difficulty in passing the examination, though I had been told that it was very difficult and that under no circumstances would I be granted a first-grade certificate. This did not prove true, however, for even though I had had no experience as a teacher I was given a first-grade certificate. This was in early September, and my school did not open till about the middle of October, so I immediately secured work on the farm of Mr. L.B. Walthall, a white neighbour, it being the harvesting season. In this community, as in most other country communities, everybody knew everybody's else business, or thought he did. It was therefore soon known throughout the community that I had returned from school and secured a first-grade certificate, and that the county superintendent, Mr. Irving, a lawyer, had also spoken several times to groups of people on the streets of the town of Farmville and other places of the excellent record I had made in my examination; indeed that he had felt obliged to grant me a first-grade certificate even though I had had no practical experience as a teacher. I think I must have shocked the whole district by working as a day labourer on a farm after having been appointed to teach. It thoroughly upset the residents, white and coloured. No coloured teacher in that locality had up to that time ever been known to do such a thing. Many white friends, also neighbours, who had heard of it mostly through coloured people, rode over to Mr. Walthall's place to see if the rumour were really true. I was a sort of curiosity, but deep down in the heart of the people I am sure that there was a feeling of genuine satisfaction that I was doing this. Mr. Walthall, who was one of the leading farmers in that section, did not hesitate to express his approval in no uncertain terms.

The following Sunday I appeared at Macedonia Baptist Church where

I previously had had charge of the Sunday School, choir, and other activities. The old minister, Brother Armstead Berkeley, while he took a text, talked more about me than anything else. He likened me to Paul, the tent maker, and a great many more extravagant comparisons were made, much to my own embarrassment. I was pleased at the beginning of his discourse, but would have been happier had he said much less about me.

Mr. Walthall, after the first few days, increased my pay to nearly twice what he was paying the others, saying that he felt that I was worth more than they. Furthermore, he did not hesitate to tell all of his men about it, and after two weeks gave me entire charge of the squad of some twenty people. The truth of the matter is I was earning more on the farm than I did later when I began teaching.

On the Sunday in October prior to the opening of school on Monday, I attended church services at Midway Baptist Church, a short distance from the school, where a large audience had gathered. It had been announced, it seems, in the town on Saturday—and almost everyone went to Farmville on Saturday from the four counties, as they do now — that the teacher would be present and speak. I was introduced by the pastor, an old friend and former night-school teacher, the Rev. Anthony G. Green. He knew of my early boyhood, and did not hesitate, in his kindly and well-meaning way, to paint the most graphic picture of me that his limited vocabulary could command. I made a short talk, and among other things urged the people to send their children to school the next day. I was early at the schoolhouse the following morning, swept up the building and cleaned the grounds. The few neighbours, seeing what I was doing, insisted upon my permitting them to do it. They thought the teacher had no business to be cleaning up the school grounds and cutting down weeds and such things. I permitted them to help me until the time came to open school.

At nine o'clock we opened. Six pupils were registered the first day. The number continued to increase rapidly until shortly afterward there were somewhere near one hundred and fifty. The schoolhouse was a two-room building, so I made application to the school board for an assistant teacher, which application was granted. The superintendent sent a young man by the name of Eston Hembricks. Mr. Hembricks was a very excellent man and not a bad teacher from the standpoint of the conventional methods of that day. He believed in whipping, and that vigorously. If a student missed three words in spelling or read poorly, or did not know his lessons, there was only one thing to follow and that whipping. In this we did not agree, and had many heated arguments over the point. I felt that it might perhaps be necessary to whip one or two, but the general upsetting of the school by having a boy take off his coat and vest, the screaming and the howling, with many of the girls also crying while the boys were being whipped, all this to my mind was generally demoralizing, and besides it grated very much on my sensibilities. He was persistent, however, in his idea that I could never maintain control of one hundred and fifty children by the method I was advocating.

The school was located in what was from many points of view a very promising community. It contained a large number of coloured people and but few white families. Very many of the coloured people owned their homes; at least they owned the land, and many of them considerable land. They had reached what is sometimes called now "the land period" in their development. They had not, however, reached "the home period." Many men who owned a hundred or more acres of land would be living in a cabin which could be built in those days for twenty-five dollars; yet these people had very high aspirations. They wanted their children educated; they were strong in their religious convictions and had fairly good churches. They were generous toward their lodges and toward religious and educational matters.

Mr. Hembricks persistently continued in the use of corporal punishment in his room in spite of my advice to the contrary. Frequently he disturbed the order in my room with the disorder which he created by his vigorous method of discipline, until, as principal teacher, I felt obliged to insist that if there were any occasion for discipline, it must be referred to me. Not being in sympathy with my method of school management, he said after a time that he would appeal the matter to the school board, and if they did not sustain him, he would resign. I was not sure how the matter would impress the school board, so I thought it wise to call together a deacon of the church and a few older men in conference with Hembricks and myself at my boarding place on a certain night. My landlady's husband, though he could neither read nor write, was a remarkably clever man. He was the political boss of the Randolph district and the leader in whatever matters concerned Negroes. Whatever happened, whether in school, in church, in politics, in secret societies, or elsewhere, must have Charlie Palmer's approval. He suggested, because of my youth and inexperience, that I leave the matter entirely in his hands. I readily acquiesced in his suggestion and he in his own way began making preparations for a big supper. He made out the bill of fare. I need not specify here the delicacies, but we had all kinds of food common to a rural coloured community of the day: opossum, raccoon, turkey, and all the delectable parts of the hog. Indeed we had, as we thought, everything that one could wish, both to eat and to drink. Instead of about seven or eight men, however, Charlie Palmer had about fifty men with about half as many women, who were not invited to the party but were present to look after the preparation and serving of the food. It was a rather warm and beautiful moonlight night. They barbecued a pig over coals in the yard, and there was a barrel of persimmon beer, of which the people drank freely, and I think that barrel had some ingredients in it other than persimmon juice. Anyhow, after we had eaten and drunk our fill and our friend Palmer had told us many a marvellous story of his experiences, political and otherwise, and had made a strong speech, advising the people to use all the influence they possessed for Prof. John M. Langston, a coloured man, who had bolted the regular Republican ticket and was running for Congress on an independent ticket in the 4th District, Judge Arnold being the regular Republican candidate, he called on me to give my ideas of Mr. Langston and why the coloured people, though they lived in the 10th Congressional District across the river from the 4th District, should use all the influence they could muster for his election. Of course I have no idea now what I said, but my words urging the importance of having a Negro representative in Congress and my criticism of many white Republicans who had gotten into office on the Negro vote and simply used us, created among the crowd a profound sensation. They yelled and threw up their hats. Some took me on their shoulders and carried me around the premises and were withal so demonstrative that I was confused and puzzled; and I am not sure even yet whether it was not the effect of the persimmon beer and other things which were very freely dispensed rather than my speech which caused this embarrassing demonstration. Then Mr. Palmer called on Hembricks for a speech. Mr. Hembricks made a good speech, but the enthusiasm had expended itself somewhat, so that while he got some applause, it was very weak by contrast. When he concluded Mr. Palmer said that it had been a meeting in which we had stressed the importance of Negroes working together under coloured leadership, and he thought it was a great mistake in any man who pretended to be a leader among coloured people to take any difficulty arising between them to white officials to settle if it could possibly be avoided. He said that the Cottontown school had had less disorder that year under its new teachers than at any time since the school was established. The children were more enthusiastic about attending school, and the homes of these children had already felt the influence of promptness and order which the pupils had been taught during the short time the school had been in session. This speech was followed by several others of the group in the same strain. The meeting broke up and the people went home. Nothing was said about the controversy between the teachers. I went to bed and Mr. Hembricks spent the night with the Palmers. He and Mr. Palmer talked late into the night. At breakfast next morning Hembricks apologized for his attitude and assured me there would be no further trouble so far as he was concerned, and from that time on I continued to handle the discipline of the school, except in cases where I thought Mr. Hembricks himself ought to handle it. No more pupils were whipped and we had a very orderly set of children. More than two hundred and fifty were enrolled during the year till we had to select, after securing the approval of the chairman of the board, two of our more advanced pupils to help us in the work.

In this locality there were four coloured churches—Greencreek, Mount Nebo, Cornerstone, and the Midway Baptist. Midway was nearest to the school. Fortunately they held services not oftener than twice a month, so that Mr. Hembricks and I could attend each church at least monthly. We were always expected to speak and to teach a Sunday-School class, if not to review the lesson. From this I am sure I got a great deal more than the scholars. It was in many ways an easy matter in this section for a Negro teacher to win the respect and confidence of the people. I have never found any group of people more willing to be led than were the people of this community. I am not sure now as to the quality or character of my teaching at the time. I doubt if it would pass muster under the eye of a modern pedagogue. I was somewhat original perhaps in some of my ideas and methods, and I introduced many things which in those days were entirely new. For instance, they had never observed Thanksgiving Day prior to my coming, so that year we had a great celebration. The pastor permitted us to use the church and people came from as far as twenty miles to be present. Some of the men who were interested in horses arranged a tournament, and at night we had chorus singing. The school sang as a body and I insisted that all the girls should appear in white dresses with blue sashes and every boy have a white sash.

I suppose I did this because I wanted to be sure that the pupils should look different from the other people present. There must have been two thousand persons on the grounds, perhaps more, and all thoroughly enjoyed the occasion.

Then at Christmas we had something of the same sort of celebration, with a Christmas tree, which was the first seen in that community. We had perhaps a dozen preachers present at this Christmas celebration. Each one had some part in the service. This way of observing the day was in striking contrast to what had been previously in vogue. Christmas in that part of Virginia, as in many other parts of the South, had been given over very largely to dissipation of one kind or another; fireworks and also "fire water" were much in evidence, and many who did not have fireworks used guns or anything that they could muster with which to make a noise. Any form of disorder was permissible. They used to sing, as I remember, a song which went like this:

> In the Summer roasting ears,
> In the Fall, "punkin",
> Christmas comes but once a year,
> And everyone must do somethin'.

The "somethin'" meant something noisy and out of the ordinary. I introduced the general singing of plantation melodies among the people, and at three o'clock each Friday afternoon we had public exercises. Often the schoolhouse could not accommodate the crowds that attended — scores of mothers and many fathers, as well as many of the white neighbours who came from long distances to hear the singing and to witness the other exercises by the children. The Negro farmers as well as the whites were much pleased with my talks once a week on general farming, poultry raising, care of cattle and hogs, the rotation of crops, and the importance of gardens, especially winter gardens. At these Friday exercises we also talked to the parents and older children on habits and manners, and many other simple, but, as we thought, needful things regarding the home, backyards, outhouses, and similar topics. We called in, too, on several occasions, leading white men to talk to the pupils on Friday evening, and each coloured preacher had a turn before the year was out. I tried to dignify the occasion by calling it the "Friday afternoon lecture."

I somehow succeeded during that year in making a very pleasant impression on the school officials: the superintendent, Mr. Corson, and the members of the precinct board. They took much pride in visiting the school, and the superintendent urged many coloured teachers to come, and brought with him, on one or two occasions, some of his white teachers. He generally called up a few classes and gave them certain examinations, and after the first visit always asked that we sing for him. We had rehearsed the pupils in singing, and the girls we had taught certain very simple gymnastic exercises and they usually went through these for his benefit. We would then have the students sing plantation melodies, which they did with a will and which, by the way, the pupils enjoyed as much as any one. As I think of it now, I wonder why they ever came or why there was any enthusiasm over these talks, and the other things that we did, for in many ways I really knew very little about what I was attempting to do.

While I learned comparatively little about scientific agriculture during my stay at Hampton, I had absorbed something of the agricultural atmosphere from Mr. Albert Howe, than whom Hampton has never had a more faithful worker. Mr. Howe gave us frequent talks on agriculture, the importance of gardens, poultry-raising, and other subjects, so that I was able, it seems, in spite of my lack of agricultural training, to help a community that knew so much less than I did.

It was a very busy year but I managed to find time for reading and study. I had had up to that time a more or less vague desire to study law. I had an idea that perhaps some day I might follow that profession, so the superintendent of schools for Prince Edward County, whose office was in Farmville nine miles away, was kind enough to give me lessons in law and lend me such of his books as I needed. He declined to accept any pay but allowed me to work in his office on Saturdays, copying deeds, contracts, and similar work, which saved time for him and was, of course, excellent training for me. This enabled me to occupy my evenings in a more or less definite, systematic way. On Saturdays when I came to town he frequently catechized me very minutely on various phases of the week's work which he had given me to do.

The following spring, Mr. Irwin, the superintendent, told me I had sufficient knowledge to pass the bar examination. It was the law in Virginia then that a candidate for the bar could receive a certificate to practice after examination by two circuit judges. I never shall forget the time I appeared before Judge Frank Irving, the father of Mr. Irving under whom I had been reading law during the winter. I had come to the court-room late one afternoon. There must have been thirty people there, many attorneys among them. The cases had all been disposed of for the term. The judge was swapping stories with some of the attorneys. He finally turned to me and said, "By the way, Moton, I understand that you want to take an examination to practice law." I told him that I did, and he said, "I might as well examine you now." I told him I was not prepared to be examined then, that I would prefer to be given another appointment. He said, "No, I can refuse you a certificate now as well as any time. I have had only one Negro in my court and he did not belong there. He was permitted to practice by courtesy, so I will examine you now. Come up here." I was certainly unprepared, but I thought I might as well face the ordeal. His son who sat over within the enclosure gave me some encouragement by saying, "You had better come over and try it anyhow. Many men have failed and you will have company."

I remember that the judge asked me to tell him first what a "demurrer" was. I undertook to tell him. He differed with me. I argued with him. In ten minutes I had forgotten that I was arguing with "His Honour," so we argued the "demurrer" in all its phases until dark. All the attorneys remained and were intensely amused, apparently. After we had spent perhaps two hours and a half in arguing this, the only question that the judge asked me, he said, "I will give you a certificate. Call up at the office tomorrow morning." And turning to the clerk of the court he said, "Write him a certificate, Claxton, and I will sign it tomorrow."

But I had to pass another examination, before a judge who was reported to be much more gruff than this one. A few days later I drove fifteen miles to the home of this other circuit judge, who lived in another county. I reached the house at breakfast time, somewhere around seven o'clock, just as the bell rang for him to come in to breakfast with the family. He saw me drive up, asked what my business was, whether I had had breakfast, and other questions. I assured him that I had had a very early breakfast and told him what my errand was. He gave me a seat on the front porch and went in to breakfast. Presently the cook came out with a tray on which was a very good breakfast, with steaming hot biscuits and other appetizing dishes. I did not send it back.

Later the judge came out and apparently in a very indifferent manner, talked of many things and asked many questions, not at all along the line of the law, as I had expected. The fact is, I was all prepared for this examination. I was prepared to give the definition of law, something of the history of law, the various divisions of the law, and to answer the questions likely to be asked. I was prepared to make up briefs, indictments, and everything else that I had been able to find after much study in law books;

but the judge asked about President Cleveland, who was then president; what I thought of him, of Congress, the tariff, the Republican Party, Mr. Lincoln, the Secession Movement. He asked my opinion of General Lee, General Jackson, and General Grant. He asked questions about Hampton Institute, General Armstrong, the relation of the races, as well as many other subjects. A famous case was then pending in an adjoining county; he asked me about the merits and demerits of both sides. It so happened that I was familiar with the case. He had seen me in the courtroom a few weeks before when he was the presiding judge. He asked me what I thought of the arguments of the opposing attorneys, and I did not hesitate to pick flaws in them and commend what I thought to be their good points. I also told him I thought one of the attorneys had been very unwise in one of the questions he had asked his client, almost losing his case himself, in my judgment. The judge expressed no opinion whatsoever. Finally he excused himself a moment, went into the house, and came back and handed me a certificate. I came away with a sense of disappoint that here I had been handed a license to practice law and had never been properly examined. I decided, therefore, to continue my studies, but as I think of it now I can understand that the examination, while technically deficient from my viewpoint, was in every sense adequate from the standpoint of this experienced jurist.

The apparent success which came to me that year brought many thoughts to my mind with reference to what I should do when I had finished my course at Hampton. Cumberland County and Cottontown—the name by this time had been changed to Adriance—seemed to me an ideal place for a small industrial school on the Hampton plan. Within a radius of perhaps ten or fifteen miles there were concentrated something like three or four thousand coloured people who could buy land, and many of whom had already secured substantial holdings. The white people were very kindly disposed toward them and anxious to sell land to coloured people. Also there were four churches. In every way it was an ideal community for a little school; so I got some of the more thoughtful coloured men together and we went over a scheme for such a school. I called on some of the leading white people and they also approved the plan, offering their support, and one gentleman offered to give ten acres of land. The county superintendent, Mr. Corson, assured us that the county would do at least as much as it had been doing, and he felt sure that they would provide the salary for the teacher. I wrote General Armstrong at Hampton and Miss

Mary F. Mackie and some others of my Hampton teachers, setting forth my plans. They strongly advised against it, and urged me to return to the Institute and to complete my course. Some of them wrote me frankly that I did not have sufficient education to undertake such a work. One lady teacher, Mrs. I.N. Tillinghast, who is at present a warden at Vassar College, wrote me very frankly that my education was exceedingly deficient; that I did not know enough about any one thing to succeed; that I had the ability to get up before a crowd and to make a certain kind of show, but that there was not nearly so much to what I was doing as I thought. I shall always remember that letter, for her argument, though hard to accept, was convincing. I therefore decided for the present, at least, to abandon the scheme.

The public-school term was five months, but with the coöperation of the parents, Mr. Hembricks and I were successful in lengthening it by two months. I shall never forget the school closing "Exhibition"—the large audience of coloured people, the wonderful dinner in the churchyard, or the committee of coloured citizens that waited on me, saying that the people had offered to double my salary the next year if I would come back. There was also a letter from the county superintendent endorsed by the chairman of the County School Board, Mr. Norton Flippin, in which they agreed that I could have the school in Cumberland County as long as they were in office. The parting there was much like the one previously described on my leaving home for Hampton.

The following summer I went to Philadelphia and succeeded in securing work in John Wanamaker's store, through the kindness of a friend who gave me a letter of introduction to Mrs. Robert C. Ogden. This, too, was a very interesting experience. I worked in what was called the housekeeping department for the first two months with a gang of about fifty men. There were but two coloured men, of whom I was one. The others were mostly Irishmen and Italians, but there were also two Dutchmen and two or three American white men. We had all of the noon hour and other off-hours when we had a chance to discuss many very interesting questions from different points of view. I never knew before that white men had so much fault to find with other white men. These men complained of the trusts, were down on both the Democratic Party and the Republican Party, as well as on Mr. Wanamaker, who was then the Postmaster General under President Harrison. It was hard for me to understand how these men could be working for a firm that gave what seemed to me so much consideration to its employees, and yet be so bitter against every person in authority. Mr. Wanamaker had just called together all of his employee who had been in the service more than ten years and presented each of them with a purse; and several of the men in our group were among this number; yet these very men were more bitter in their criticism afterward than before. We saw Mr. Wanamaker occasionally on Saturday and sometimes on Monday mornings. Mr. Robert C. Ogden, the manager, we saw daily. It was rather interesting to me to observe, that the Irish and the native Americans of the group were generally the most outspoken in their denunciation of the rich and of all office holders. The Italians said very little, and the Dutchmen said nothing unless their opinion was asked. Later in the summer I was transferred to the Bureau of Information, where I remained until the middle of September, when I left Philadelphia for Hampton.

Chapter 6

Ending Student Days

HAVING had my year at teaching, as required by the course at Hampton, I was now eligible for membership in the Senior Class. I began my work in October, 1889. Of the seventy-eight students who had been promoted to the Senior Class with me, only forty-eight returned to complete the course. I had reached the rank of captain in the Middle Year; but things had somewhat changed during my fifteen months away from the school. Mr. George L. Curtis, who as commandant had been most kind and friendly to me, had resigned his position and Mr. Charles W. Freeland had succeeded him. I was not sure that I would receive as much consideration from Mr. Freeland as I had from Mr. Curtis. In fact, I was reasonably sure that I would not, because the boys had already prejudiced my mind against him. He was an Episcopal minister and they said he came from Georgia, and was much worse, as we understood it, than a real Georgian, because, as they said, he was a "re-constructed Northerner." The idea was prevalent then as now among coloured people that when Northern people come South and change from the Northern to the Southern attitude on the race question they are much more intolerant, from the Negro's point of view, than native Southerners. My prejudice against him therefore was very strong, and I had about reached the conclusion that he and I could never get along together. All of us had some resentment against General Armstrong for having brought such a person into the work. The young men did not hesitate to express the opinion that if General Armstrong meant to have a Southerner he should have gotten a *real* Southerner, and if he were going to have a Northerner he ought to have a *real* Northerner. It so happened that several boys from Savannah, Georgia, where Mr. Freeland had had a parish, entered school that fall, and those young men, I noticed, spoke very well of him and of his mother. They said he had been very popular with the coloured people in Savannah and with white people also. This report had to some extent the effect of allaying what was growing to be considerable bitterness on the part of the students generally. I soon found, however, that, while Mr. Freeland was very strict and very exacting, he was most kind and generous and that students who lived up to his rules had no difficulty in getting on with him.

When I entered Hampton in 1885, except for a slight inclination toward the legal profession, I did not have any very definite plan or notion as to what I wanted to do, but I was clear in the desire to return home and continue in the same activities in the school, church, and other local movements in which I had engaged before going off to school. My thought was to get sufficient education to do these things better and to save myself the embarrassment which I frequently underwent because I did not know as much as many people in the community thought I did. But when I entered the Senior Class my mind was pretty definitely set on the legal profession, and though I had passed the examination and been licensed to practice in Virginia, and while the teachers at Hampton did not oppose my plan exactly, they did raise the question freely and frankly, and I might add frequently also, as to whether I could thus render my people the greatest service, and whether legal advice at that time was the greatest need of an uneducated, struggling people in the rural districts of the South.

There was never any question, even from my earliest youth, I think, as to my desire to be helpful to my people, but exactly how it should be done was not wholly clear. My heart was pretty definitely set on going back to Prince Edward County, and the little town of Farmville was to me an ideal place. Something about the atmosphere of the locality appealed very strongly to me. I had been in Philadelphia, Washington, and Baltimore, and had seen a little of Norfolk, Richmond, and Petersburg, but somehow they did not compare in importance to my mind with Farmville, nor seem nearly so attractive as a place to live in as this little town on the Appomattox River.

It was the custom of Mr. Frissell to study with the Seniors the International Sunday-School Lessons. His custom was to take up the lesson a Sunday ahead of the calendar because most of the members of the Senior Class taught in the neighbouring Sunday Schools, churches, jail, poorhouse, and the two or three mission Sunday Schools in the county which were under the direct supervision of the Institute. The Seniors always looked forward with a great deal of pleasant anticipation to being in Mr. Frissell's class, because his reputation as a teacher of the Bible was well known among the student body as well as among the teachers. During the last half of the year it was General Armstrong's custom to take up with the Senior Class Dr.

Mark Hopkins's book, "The Outline Study of Man." He never called it psychology until usually about the last week of the school term and then he would announce to the class that they had been studying psychology. I can remember very little now of any particular thing that I learned from the textbook during the four and a half months, but I doubt if there is a single member of that class today who does not feel even now the power and influence of General Armstrong's earnest, strong, forceful, inspiring personality and the simple illustrations which he used to drive home the telling points he made. He brought out of the lessons the importance of proper relations between black people and white people, and the value of being able to approach and deal with a person when you knew he did not like you and was prejudiced against you; how we ourselves, who were not without strong prejudices, even race prejudices, could deal fairly with people against whom we had prejudice, members of our own race as well as of other races. He never failed—as was also true of Mr. Frissell and the other teachers—to emphasize the importance of engaging in such work as would be of the largest benefit to the coloured race, and he never expressed any doubt as to the final triumph of right and justice and the ultimate success of the two races in adjusting the difficult and very-much-talked-of "race problem." Before the close of the year a large majority of the members of the class, Indians as well as Negroes, had pretty definitely made up their minds that they would engage in some work that would have a direct bearing on the development of their races.

Being the ranking captain, besides filling other places of responsibility in the school, somehow or other I was able to gain the confidence of most of the student body. I was made president of the Young People's Christian Association, an organization nominally under the chaplain, Mr. Frissell, but it took in all of the religious organizations of the school, the officers being elected by the student body. I was also made president of the Old Dominion Debating Society, the Boys' Glee Club, and the Senior Class, as well as president of the Temperance Society. These honours carried with them, of course, certain responsibilities which I rather shrank from because I did not wish to have anything hamper my studies. In former years my class work had been somewhat along the lines of previous reading, but the Senior work was almost entirely new, except perhaps general history in which I had had no systematic instruction. Owing to this fact it was necessary for me to give closer attention to my studies than ever before.

I recall that after my election as president of the Temperance Society one of my very kind teachers, Miss Davis, to whom I have previously referred, met me as we came down from the assembly room, and calling me into her classroom said, "Moton, I hope you won't accept any other office. It would be very bad for you; a number of your friends among the teachers are afraid that your head is going to be turned; because you are receiving too much attention." While this was somewhat of a shock to me I received it with good grace, because, as my Sunday-School teacher, I had learned to value her opinions, though they were often expressed with embarrassing frankness. I carried my new honours as best I knew how, and had to face no serious difficulties, for as a matter of fact most of the details were looked after by the teachers, who were on the administrative committees of many of these organizations.

At Christmas time there was an occurrence that tested the character of many of us to the utmost. Two nights before Christmas the young men had been permitted to escort the young women home from a concert in the gymnasium. Everyone was happy and prepared to enjoy the usual Hampton Christmas. If anything, we had made more elaborate preparations that year than usual. General Armstrong had invited some very distinguished guests for the holidays, among them General Morgan, Commissioner of Indian Affairs, with Mrs. Morgan and a party of friends from Washington. Dr. Washburn, the head of Robert College in Constantinople, had brought down a party of foreign missionaries and there were many other distinguished guests. An unusual effort had been made by the general committee on athletics, and it had been planned that the social gatherings should be of a high order. The programmes for the debating societies and other organizations had been arranged with much care. Each holiday night had been carefully planned for. As we left the gymnasium after the Christmas concert, each young man escorting a young woman, we were stopped after we got about half-way between the gymnasium and Virginia Hall by one of the matron's assistants. I was leading the line. We walked up to two ladies, one of whom was the matron's assistant, and who stood in the middle of the road, a narrow passageway between one of the buildings and a laundry fence, as I remember, so that it was not easy to pass without brushing them aside. One lady remarked, "We did not understand that you were to escort the young women home tonight." I replied that it was the custom to do so and nothing had anyone said to the contrary. She said, "Well, we will escort them the rest of the way." I thereupon promptly excused myself to the young woman and left, and every other man who passed along, and there must have been about two hundred, separated from the young woman whom he accompanied, except a few who refused to leave.

The next morning some eight or ten men crowded into my room before breakfast, demanding that I take the initiative in getting suitable reparation for the humiliation which we had suffered the night before. Though I felt the humiliation as keenly as any one, and did not hesitate so to express myself, I saw at once that those young men were in no mood to listen to reason from any one. I suggested that after breakfast we get together about twenty-five young men representing every class in the school and also the Indian students and go over the matter. They did not take kindly to that suggestion, but they argued the case considerably, and finally the majority decided against my proposal. At breakfast time James R. Spurgeon, now a lawyer in Brooklyn, New York, and for a time after his graduation Secretary to the United States Legation in Liberia, read a notice in the dining room calling a meeting of all of the young men immediately after breakfast. I felt that the indignation speeches which were likely to be made in that meeting might stir the boys to do almost anything, the resentment of the evening before being very strong. There were quite a few, however, especially the older fellows, who agreed with me. I did not go to the meeting but a committee waited on me a few moments after the students assembled and demanded my presence; so I went.

Spurgeon was the temporary chairman, and called the meeting to order with a fiery introductory speech. He was then and is now an able orator. I was nominated and unanimously elected chairman over my very strong protest. I insisted that I would not serve. In declining I had the chance to say some things I could not otherwise have said. I told them I would accept the chairmanship only on condition that the decisions of the chair should be strictly observed. I used the opportunity to make an appeal to the cooler heads among them to do nothing for which they would afterward be ashamed. They agreed and I accepted. Following the perfecting of the permanent organization many exciting speeches were made. The indignation of the boys was tremendous. I realized that I was facing four hundred very determined young men, who did not quite know what to do but were determined to do something. One resolution which immediately met with popular favour was to the effect that all cooks, milkers, stablemen, and workers in every department, boys and girls, would strike for the holiday period. In this the girls, who felt as strongly in the matter as the young men and were waiting on the other side of the grounds for the decision, heartily concurred. This motion was going through, but before putting it I left the stand, asking my classmate, Spurgeon, to occupy the chair, while I took the floor. I hoped first to put Spurgeon in a position where he could not argue against me. I raised the question as to the wisdom of having the cooks and waitresses and waiters and milkers stop during the week and called attention to the fact that however angry we might be we had to eat and though the boys might go to near-by restaurants, there were two or three hundred girls who could not. I raised the question as to the common sense of having the cattle and other animals suffer, calling attention to the fact that they had not committed any crime and that it would be a shame not to feed them or care for them. I suggested that a committee be appointed to wait on General Armstrong. It was clear that that suggestion would not be accepted. I then offered an amendment: that we refuse to attend any socials during the week, but that we would urge every student to perform all official duties, such as attending prayers and performing our work and school duties, pointing out that to stay away from the social functions would be just as effective, indeed much more so, and would give no ground for any "come-back" at us as a student body or individuals.

This suggestion appealed to the majority of the boys very strongly. A Sioux Indian, John Bruyier, offered an amendment to my amendment, as did also another classmate, James H. Phillips — now a successful business man in Montgomery, Alabama, who was then as now a clear, forceful, and effective speaker — to the effect that no teacher or official of the school should know of this decision, that notices would be given and arrangements made for all social and literary functions as usual. In their judgment the two amendments combined would be sufficiently effective in teaching the Faculty the lesson, which we thought they needed to learn, about "insulting ladies and gentlemen without cause." In the end these amendments were carried and a solemn pledge taken that no person should repeat our decision outside of that meeting, except to the committee of girls, and that if any man appeared at any one of these functions he would be dealt with appropriately and his life in the school made so miserable that it would be impossible for him to remain.

This action was reported to the girls, who met and quietly and quickly passed similar resolutions. At evening prayers the week's programme was announced. Everyone sat quietly. There was to be an entertainment that evening and various class gatherings. A committee was appointed to see that no student entered any of these places, perchance any one had not understood. To only one place did any students go—two boys who had not heard of the action got in before the guard who had been assigned to that place arrived at his station. The next day it was clearly understood what the feeling of the student body was, and for the rest of the week the holiday programme was abandoned. It was evident to all concerned that the students had resented what was considered a very serious infringement on their "rights." The teachers felt very badly; and we, ourselves felt that the holidays had been very dull and dreary, but we all found ample compensation in the fact that we had "disciplined" the officials of the Institute. To be sure we deprived ourselves, of what we had looked forward to as an unusually gay Christmas, even for Hampton, and I rather think we lost more in this direction than the teachers. I often think now that people who have to do with student bodies sometimes forget the bitter resentment that students feel for certain "indignities," as they regard them; that they are too often inclined to forget the feelings of students and consider them as unimportant, forgetting what they did and felt when they themselves were students. Out of such incidents, when properly handled, students sometimes can get more real education as to how to meet life's problems than perhaps in a year of the ordinary conventional schooling.

Chapter 7

Black, White, and Red

ON A Saturday night just before the close of school, General Armstrong invited the Senior boys to spend an evening at his home. He told some fascinating stories of his war experiences with Negro soldiers, the Ninth U.S. Coloured Troops which he recruited and commanded at the Battle of Gettysburg. He showed us his uniform with a colonel's shoulder straps, which his mother had just sent on to him from California, together with his sword. He told with frankness of the weaknesses which he had observed in Negro soldiers and of their strong points as well, but he showed clearly, though apparently unconsciously, what wonderful growth these men made under kind yet positive discipline. We had a most interesting and instructive evening. As the party was leaving, he asked me to remain for a few moments, saying that he wished to speak with me. I supposed, of course, that he wished me to do some errand for him, but to my great surprise he began by asking what my plans were for the future. I told him something of what had been on my mind with regard to the school plan for Cumberland County and my desire to help those people who had been so responsive to and appreciative of my year's work, and who were very desirous of having me return, for throughout the year I had been receiving letters from committees as well as individuals urging me to come back. He commended the scheme and pointed out very clearly how it could be done, what a good thing it would be, how we could work in coöperation with Hampton and bring students to a certain degree of academic as well as industrial development, fitting them for entrance into the Junior Class, at Hampton, he thought, without examination. He also pointed out many essential details which I had overlooked. While in a general way he heartily approved of the plan, he nevertheless strongly advised against my undertaking it for at least a year. He did not hesitate to tell me that I needed more experience, and suggested that I could be very much more useful to my race and would conduct my school in a very much more satisfactory way if I would remain at Hampton for he present and help in the training of teachers for the large number of public schools that were being opened up throughout Virginia and the South. He would accept no decision at that time; in fact, he did not give me much chance to say anything. He simply took for granted what I would do and how I should do it. "You can think this over," he said, "and let me know if there is any reason why you should not take up your duties at the close of school as assistant to Mr. Freeland, the commandant of the school cadets."

I took General Armstrong's suggestion and accepted work at Hampton as assistant to the commandant, but decided not to enter upon my duties until the opening of school. I therefore again secured work through Mr. Robert C. Ogden, then in the John Wanamaker store at Philadelphia. In the meantime, it seemed advisable that Mr. Freeland, the commandant, should go out through the Indian country and select Indian students for Hampton, this custom having obtained ever since Captain (now General) Robert H. Pratt brought on the first party of Indians in 1878 It was Captain Pratt who, after serving for a short time at Hampton with the Indians, founded the famous Carlisle School over which he successfully presided for many years.

Mr. Freeland's absence made it desirable for me to begin work at Hampton in the summer as acting commandant in charge of the three hundred or more Negro and Indian boys. Mr. Ogden readily released me from my engagement, saying that he always doubted the wisdom of the Hampton graduates coming North so soon after graduation, for fear the fascination of Northern city life would incline them to remain, and congratulated me that I had escaped this temptation. I took up quarters in the "Wigwam," the building in which the Indian boys were housed. General Armstrong used to call the person who lived in the building the "House Father." It so happened also that one of the teachers who had been engaged to teach in the Indian school for the summer was obliged to resign her position because of illness, so I was asked to fill her place.

While I had, during my four years, been in more or less intimate contact with Indian students on the parade ground, in classroom, dining room, and elsewhere, and had some very intimate friends among the young men, I had never before taught Indian pupils, neither had I gotten a very clear insight into the Indian's attitude and viewpoint on matters in general. I learned for the first time how different it was from my own. I was surprised to find how hard it was for many Indians to adapt themselves to the customs of the white man, for they thought the old way, their way, better and in many cases gave very good reasons to support their view. Their opinion, for example, about the white man's religion was that he preached one thing and frequently practiced another; that he preached human brotherhood, for instance, while very few whites, so far as the Indians could observe, actually practiced human brotherhood. This thought was firmly fixed in the minds of many of them. This was a new experience for a Negro, for while many of us shared this view about the inconsistencies of the white man and how far he was from actually practicing his religion, we had nevertheless adapted ourselves to the white man's ways, and had, consciously or unconsciously, and sometimes anxiously, absorbed the white man's civilization. The nearer we came to it, it seemed, the happier we were. I learned for the first time that other peoples than the Negro had problems and race feelings and prejudices, and learned to sympathize with another race, one, too, that was more nearly on a plane with my own and whose difficulties and handicaps seemed much greater than those of my own race. Living in the building with the Indian boys and being in their prayer meetings, and often acting as pitcher on their baseball team, along with contact in the Sunday School and in the day school classes of boys and girls, all gave me occasion to study more or less minutely the Indian character, especially by way of contrast with the Negro.

I had taught Sunday School at intervals during my entire school career in one of the neighbouring coloured schools, and I remember with what enthusiasm my immature Biblical interpretations were received by the pupils and how comparatively easy it was to drive home a Bible lesson from every-day life. Not so with the Indians, however. They agreed that the point was well taken, but frequently I would find some pupil raising his hand—sometimes a girl who, I thought, was paying no attention to what was going on—and she would ask why Christian white people had cheated the Indians. Such interruptions, of course, frequently took all of the "wind out of my untrimmed sails."

In this connection, I remember that General Nelson A. Miles, then major-general of the United States Army on an official inspection of Fortress Monroe, sent up to say that he would inspect the cadets at Hampton on Sunday morning. During this inspection, as the adjutant read the orders for the day, General Miles heard the name of "Paul Natchee" and asked if Natchee came from Fort Sill and if he had been at Mount Vernon barracks. He was told that he had. The General then said, "This is the son of the old

Chief Natchee whom, I am sorry to relate, I was obliged to kill because of his persistent treachery." He asked how the boy was getting along and expressed a desire to see him before he left the grounds.

We then marched into the chapel and instead of the usual Sunday morning sermon, General Miles delivered a most helpful address. I had given orders to have Natchee remain after church and speak to me, which he did. I brought him up to General Miles with all of the deference due to the General's position, accompanied as he was by a large retinue of army officers and many prominent civilians as well as several naval officers, there being at that time some war vessels anchored in Hampton Roads. I presented Paul to General Miles. Extending his hand he greeted this boy of about seventeen years of age very cordially, unusually so for the ranking general of the United States Army, and in the presence, too, of a number of his subordinate officers. Paul looked him straight in the eye, did not salute, and refused to shake hands. I thought he had not observed the General's extended hand, and in a whisper I said, "The General wants to shake hands with you," but in typical Indian fashion he said, "Know it." General Miles, who had won his fame as an Indian fighter and who always observed every movement about him, turned to me and said, "Never mind, Major. He is an Indian. He will not shake hands." The General lectured him in a very kindly way on his stubbornness, telling him that his father might have been of great service to his race but for his indomitable and unconquerable stubbornness, which undoubtedly Paul had inherited. I was very much humiliated. So was Doctor Frissell. I think General Miles was the only person present who was not. I made up my mind to punish this young man very severely, and evidently General Miles knew it, though I said nothing. After I had dismissed Paul the General turned to me and said, "Do not punish him. He inherits that spirit. It can never be gotten out of him." As soon as I had an opportunity I called Paul in. When he walked into the office he said: "I ready go guard house. I stay there thousand years, never shake hands wid him. He killed my father." He broke down and wept, and through tears he murmured, "He killed my father. I never shake hands wid him. I never speak to him."

My duties included, among other things, clerical work in the commandant's office, supervision of the drills, and instruction of the battalion in military tactics. Mr. Freeland, the commandant, was a man of remarkable ability and very methodical.

I admired the ease and dispatch with which he could turn off the immense amount of work that was his, and the way in which he never permitted things to drag. I have always been grateful for my experience under him. As a matter of fact, my plans and methods of work during the twenty-five years that I served as commandant and executive officer at Hampton Institute were strongly influenced by the experience which I received during this year's contact with Mr. Freeland.

During that same year, when I was travelling with the Hampton Quartette as a singer and speaker, while en route between Albany and Boston, General Armstrong took the opportunity to ask me many rather interesting and searching questions. I had been acting as assistant disciplinarian under Mr. Freeland. I did not know whether my work had been satisfactory or not. The General among other things asked whether I thought, with the year's experience, if left entirely alone with the discipline, I could handle the situation at the school. He wanted to know if I had the organization of the battalion clearly in my mind and if I could handle it successfully. He asked me many questions about the school in general: what my attitude was; if I had noticed any differences between the races, the white, the coloured, and the Indian; if I had noticed any difference between the Northern white man and the Southern white man. He finally ended more or less abruptly by saying, "I want you to familiarize yourself very thoroughly with all phases of the work of the school, not only with reference to the discipline of the young men, but everything else that has to do with the work." I was very much disturbed because from the tone of his remarks I was rather inclined to feel that I had failed in my work.

We went on to Boston, where we spent many days holding meetings in the interest of Hampton's work. On my return to the school a few weeks later I went directly to Mr. Frissell, the chaplain, and did what everyone in the school usually did—teachers and students alike when in trouble—I asked him what General Armstrong had in his mind. I told him that I had been much disturbed by the questions which the General had asked me. He assured me that I had no need to be disturbed, that my year had been satisfactory, and that the General, as well as others, was very much pleased, so much so that he had in mind asking me to assume charge of the Department of Discipline and Military Instruction of the Institute. Mr. Freeland had resigned and General Armstrong had made up his mind to place a coloured man for the first time in this very responsible position. He said that it was believed by many that Negro students would not respond to authority from one of their own number; but that Booker Washington's success at Tuskegee Institute, and the very satisfactory way in which I had handled some delicate situations during the year between the teachers and the students, as well as between Negroes and Indians, had convinced the General, as well as himself, that there would be much less trouble and friction in the school if I were placed in charge of the discipline. I confess this was a very great surprise to me. Instead of appealing to my pride it almost frightened me that I should for a minute have been considered for such a position. On the other hand, it was not my intention to remain at Hampton for more than two years. My idea was to get the larger experience which General Armstrong had suggested in the conversation at his house the year before and then go into some pioneer work among my people. The truth is I had never given up the idea of starting the school in Cumberland County, and was also interested still in the study of law.

Mr. Frissell remarked to me in the same conversation that I seemed to be disturbed by the suggestion that had been made and at the idea of remaining at Hampton, and I reminded him that, as he knew, I had always had in mind going into some work in the rural districts and that he and General Armstrong had told me that I could be of larger service by remaining at Hampton for a while and helping General Armstrong and himself to fit students for just the kind of work that I had in mind to do.

One morning some days later I marched the boys into school, and went to the office somewhat troubled because it seemed to me the boys had drilled worse that morning than usual. I had put them through the setting-up exercises and the whole thing was most ragged and unsatisfactory. I was just making up my mind to take the whole group for what was called "extra drill" in the afternoon after school, taking their play time to see if I could not by some possibility lick them into better shape. I noticed that morning that General Armstrong and Mr. Frissell had been walking up and down the road facing the parade ground, apparently oblivious to what was going on. Nevertheless, I was anxious that the boys should make a good showing, or at least do ordinarily well. General Armstrong walked over toward me and without any preliminary remarks said, "I want you to take the responsibility of the discipline next year." Mr. Freeland, he said, had resigned, and would probably be made chaplain in the United States Army. He went on in his characteristic way telling what he wanted me to do, what improvements he thought ought to be made, and what results we ought to accomplish. I tried several times to interject a question or two but without success. He paid no attention whatever to my questions. He simply assumed that I would do it. Finally I got a word in, with Mr. Frissell's help, to the effect that I had not planned to remain at Hampton and about what I had looked forward to doing. He asked me why I wanted to go into pioneer work and I told him I thought I could best help my people that way. He said, "You want to be of the largest service to your race, do you not?" and I assured him that I did. Then he said, "Hampton is the place. Mr. Freeland be leaving in a few weeks. In the meantime, I want you to get all matters thoroughly in your own hands." I finally agreed to take the work for two years. That was in May of 1891. I entered upon my duties with full responsibility in June of the same year, and remained at the Institute during the summer. I took up my new responsibilities with considerable reluctance mainly because of the many elements that entered into it. There were many temperaments, races, and conditions that had to be dealt with. There were Northern white people and there were Southern white people on the Hampton staff; there were also coloured people, and in the student body there were young people from the North and from the South, the majority, of course, from the South. There were one hundred and fifty members of the Indian race, representing perhaps a score of different tribes, and frequently the tribal differences were as great and developed stronger feelings than racial differences

There were other nationalities represented in the student body besides the Negro and Indian: Chinese, Japanese, Africans, Armenians, Hawaiians, and others. So I entered upon the work with many misgivings as to the chances of success. I knew something of the difficulties that Mr. Curtis and Mr. Freeland had had to face in adjusting these very delicate relations, and consequently was surprised to find later on that the work, while exacting, was not so difficult as I had thought. I had from the beginning, it would appear, the cordial good will and hearty coöperation and help of almost everyone, from General Armstrong to the humblest student.

In the following November General Armstrong, while in the midst of an address near Boston, was stricken with paralysis, from which he never wholly recovered, remaining an invalid for about two years thereafter, but entering more or less actively into the school's affairs, though it was necessary for him to be moved about in a wheel-chair. During this period Mr. Frissell performed the more active duties of principal. I learned during these years to know General Armstrong very much better than ever before.

I had previously been with him much in the North, and had observed many things about him that had struck me as unusual. It was difficult to understand how a man who was always as busy as he and who lived under such continuous pressure could be always solicitous for the comfort of the young men who were with him, Negroes and Indians, for there was usually at least one Indian in the party. He looked personally into our quarters to see whether they were comfortable or not. He did the same with respect to our meals, as well as other matters affecting our welfare. Frequently it happened at railroad stations, when it was necessary to hire a hack for ourselves or wagon to carry luggage, that he picked out the man who had the poorest horse and the most dilapidated vehicle. One day when Mr. Wm. H. Daggs, who generally managed our party, questioned the wisdom of our piling into a hack which looked as if it would break down at any minute, the General remarked that he always selected the poorest horse and hack because it was evident that this man needed the money more than the others. He added, jokingly, that this might not always hold for the reason that sometimes the evidences of poverty on the part of the hackman might be due to his own prodigality.

One day in May, 1893 when he was very ill, he sent for me to come over to the Mansion House, but this was against the doctor's orders; so Mrs. Armstrong and I agreed that it was wiser for me not to see him, but he insisted upon my coming and finally she thought that perhaps it was better that I should see him. He remarked that he wanted to see me because he had noticed latterly that students, in passing his home to and from their meals, had been much quieter than previously. During his confinement to the house he had enjoyed the hearty laughter of the young men as they passed and their singing of plantation melodies and other songs. He asked me the very direct question if I had given orders that they should be more quiet because of his illness. There was no way to evade the question so I had to admit that such an order had been given. With some emphasis he said that he did not wish to have his illness affect in any way the school's activities; that he did not wish to have any change made even in the event of his death. "I want," he said, "even at my funeral that everything should be as simple as possible and that the school should be interrupted for as little time as possible"; and then he further suggested that I should arrange with Mr. Frissell's approval to have some kind of concert or pleasant entertainment or something, to relieve the depression which he was afraid his illness was causing.

This was in the early morning. In the middle of the afternoon of the same day he sent for me again to know what arrangements I had made. I understood General Armstrong well enough to know that if he suggested anything, even though he might say there was no hurry about it, in a very few hours he would either come into your office or call you into his and ask if you had done it, so I never put off carrying out any suggestion or request or order that he gave. So when he called me over to the house to know what had been done, I told him we had arranged for a baseball game the following afternoon with the dining-room men of the Hygeia Hotel. This game, as it was played by the waiters, always brought up a great many guests also from Old Point Comfort, officers as well as soldiers. The General was very much pleased with this arrangement and requested that it should be an afternoon holiday for teachers as well as students and that everything should be shut down. I could not understand how a man who was desperately ill—and of whom we were expecting every minute to hear that the end had come—could be thinking about such matters and going into the minutest details about all the affairs of the Institute, especially as they affected the life of the students. Also there were certain exceptional boys whom he knew, some who were not happy or satisfied about certain matters affecting their course of study and who had been in to see him. He wanted to know if these matters had been satisfactorily adjusted.

The following day, the 11th of May, 1893 the ball game was played. It was intensely interesting. Throughout the afternoon the grounds resounded with the tremendous shouts of the students. The playing was good on both sides. The cheering was equally loud from the visitors; for they, for the most part, were in sympathy with the waiters rather than with the students. In the midst of this tense situation, about the seventh inning, with the score standing "nothing to nothing," Mr. Frissell came down and called me aside and asked me what I thought of stopping the game, for General Armstrong had just died. He knew, he said, that the General would not want it stopped. I told him I felt sure the students would feel embarrassed to know that they had been playing under such circumstances, even though General Armstrong wished it so, and he and I agreed also that we owed something to the sentiment of the community and therefore decided that the game should be stopped.

General Armstrong's death was without doubt the most serious blow that the Institute had ever received. It was difficult for us to see how the school could exist without its founder. General Armstrong was a man of great force. His personality was so overwhelming that it seemed to me, as well as to others wiser than myself no doubt, that no one could carry on the work which he had founded and to which he had given the best twenty-five years of his life. Everybody at Hampton loved Mr. Frissell and had the greatest respect for him. He was in the confidence of teachers and students even more so than General Armstrong, but we seriously doubted whether he could carry forward the work of Hampton. In fact, many felt quite sure that he could not fill General Armstrong's place. And as I think of it today, after twenty-six years, I am convinced that we were right in feeling that neither Mr. Frissell nor any one else could be to Hampton what General Armstrong had been. General Armstrong had in a real sense completed his work, and a remarkable work it was! He had given America a new educational idea and developed a new ideal in education. He left Hampton in such condition that it could not go down, and the educational method which he worked out at Hampton could not but take a stronger hold on America and the civilized world.

In a striking way, Doctor Frissell, in the twenty-four years in which he presided at Hampton, made his work as perfect and complete as did General Armstrong; but in doing so he filled his own place, and that, too, in a way that would have met General Armstrong's approval.

One would naturally expect it to be irksome and disagreeable to ferret out irregularities, punish misdemeanors, and settle disputes, and that it would tend to create unpopularity with the student body, especially with those over whom it is necessary to assert authority. Added to this, there was the difficulty of having to deal with Indians as well as with members of my own race. Many of my friends, therefore, both white and black, told me frankly that I might succeed with my own race but that it would not be possible for me to succeed as a disciplinarian with the Indians. They felt that when questions should arise between the two races, as frequently happened, it would be difficult for me to settle them, for the Indians would naturally expect me to be partial to the Negroes, while the Negroes, on the other hand, would suspect that, to escape this criticism, I would very likely be partial to the Indians. As a consequence, they thought I would constantly be in a dilemma and would be criticized for what I did as well as for what I did not do.

I realized when I accepted the work that I would have to face difficulties, yet I also felt that if a person did his best and was honest and sympathetic in his dealings with the boys, that both Negroes and Indians would accept his decisions. During my twenty-five years in the work at Hampton I never had occasion to believe my assumption incorrect. To be sure I had to exercise discretion, especially when disputes arose between tribes or the two races; and I found that it was frequently very much better, instead of giving boys demerits for personal differences, to take the time to lead them both, if possible, to see their mistakes; and I usually found then, as I find now, that there are always two sides to a controversy. I found that it was usually worth while to take the time to bring them to the point where they would be willing to apologize each to the other. In consequence, I have always felt that much of the friction between races, as well as between nations and individuals, is due to misunderstanding, that if people would take the time to understand one another and get one another's point of view, they would frequently find that things are not so bad as they imagine.

I had from the beginning a very strong, loyal first assistant in my work among the boys, a man who as a boy worked with me at the saw-mill along with Mr. Palmer, and who at the same time was my room-mate. This was Captain Allen Washington, now Major Allen Washington, who deserves the utmost credit for his share in any success achieved in the disciplinary work at Hampton Institute for the quarter of a century during which I was responsible for it. People even now wonder and frequently ask how the two races — the Negro and the Indian — get along together at Hampton. The truth of the matter is that at Hampton there has never been any serious manifestation of unpleasant relations between the two races. There are certain racial characteristics that are unmistakable, and the two races are in some particulars as different in temperament as they are in colour.

Types more diverse could hardly have been selected than the two thus brought together at Hampton. The Negro, as we have long known, is cheerful and buoyant, emotional and demonstrative, keen of apprehension, ambitious, persistent, responsive to authority, and deeply religious. In striking contrast stands the Indian — reserved, self-contained, self-controlled, deliberate in speech and action, sensitive, distrustful, proud, and possessed of a deep sense of personal worth and dignity.

But if the differing characteristics are evident, the similarity of the two races in condition and prospects is also striking. The Negro and the Indian have both been retarded in their development, alike in economic and social progress. They lack equally the helpful influence of heredity, that tremendous moral momentum acquired only by centuries of successive and cumulative effort. They are both aspiring, the Negro with an earnestness that often outstrips his development; the Indian with a dawning realization of his needs. Both still need, as do some other races, such moral and mental discipline as will fix in them the habits of obedience, order, accuracy, application, and the many other private virtues, the habitual practice of which makes the man. The very diversities of the two races under instruction at Hampton proved, in many respects, to be helps rather than hindrances to their development. Each served in many instances as a daily lesson to the other in the problems and difficulties of life. The Negro student learned that he did not have a monopoly of the troubles incident to the effort to rise; that his is not the only race that faces a struggle in securing the rights and privileges of an advanced civilization. The Indian student saw the arts and practices of this civilization acquired and adapted by a race whose development corresponded more nearly to his own. He caught the inspiration of the manly endeavour and sturdy self-reliance that have characterized the Indian graduates of Hampton in all their subsequent endeavours among their own people. Through all my contact of thirty-one years as student and worker at Hampton it became increasingly apparent that the ground of racial adjustment lies, not in the emphasis of faults and of differences between races, but rather in the discovery of likenesses and of virtues which make possible their mutual understanding and coöperation.

Soon after General Armstrong's death and Doctor Frissell's election to the principalship, he told me that he would like to have me make up my mind to remain permanently at Hampton; that he thought the position that I occupied, especially as affecting the delicate relations which obtained at Hampton between the three races as well as between the two sections of the country, was of the utmost importance and that he needed my help in carrying out the wishes of the Founder regarding Hampton's very important work for the Negro and Indian races.

Even up to this time I had not thoroughly made up my mind to remain at Hampton permanently. I was much interested in the experience I was receiving through my contact with teachers and students. I continued my work along very much the same lines as during General Armstrong's life, giving more of my time, however, to the administration of the school's affairs under Doctor Frissell's direction. I also devoted more time toward the raising of funds in the North, thereby relieving Doctor Frissell and Dr. H.B. Turner, who had succeeded Doctor Frissell as chaplain of the Institute, in some degree of the burden of raising money necessary to carry on the work of the school.

After graduating at Hampton, I felt, with many of the other resident graduates, that our education was not complete, so for several years we did postgraduate work in certain advanced subjects which had not come in our regular course. The first few years we paid for this instruction ourselves, but later the school officials felt that it was proper for them to provide teachers for this work. I also continued my law studies one evening a week under the tutelage of Mr. F.S. Collier, a lawyer in the town of Hampton, a Southern gentleman who not only gave me instruction without pay but allowed me the free use of his law library.

Through the generosity of Prof. Francis G. Peabody, I had the opportunity of attending several sessions of the Harvard Summer School, taking courses in gymnastics, English, and composition. For ten years I had continued my work practically without any let up, except for Summer School and Northern work and occasional visits among my own people in the South.

By this time some of my friends, among them Doctor Frissell, Mr. Robert C. Ogden, and Mr. Arthur Curtiss James, the latter two trustees of Hampton Institute, felt that I was very much in need of rest. They said I showed signs of fatigue, mental and physical, which I confess I had not observed. Finally, in the summer of 1901 Doctor Frissell told me that whether I wished to go or not, he and one of the trustees had arranged for me to take a trip to Europe and that this trustee would provide the means, adding that he understood that I was looking forward to a trip at some time. He gave me a few days to map out the route I would like to cover.

This whole conversation with Doctor Frissell afterward seemed almost a dream. The idea of actually going to Europe and going practically anywhere I wished to go was almost overwhelming. I mapped out what I would like to do and the countries that I would like especially to see, putting particular emphasis on southern Europe, because the Italian emigration was very large at that time and I was anxious to see another people who were more nearly on the plane of the majority of my own race in America; and then, too, I wanted to see Germany, and, of course, France and England. Doctor Frissell and the trustee referred to offered many suggestions when they knew exactly what I wished to accomplish.

Accompanied by a friend, I sailed from New York in May of the same year. After a day at the Azores we landed at Naples and came up through the principal cities of Italy into Switzerland and Germany, Belgium and France, England and Ireland. Before this I had been inclined to feel discouraged at times about my own race, and whatever people might say with reference to the advantages of the Negro in this country, I somehow felt that he was at the bottom of the scale of development, and of opportunities as well; but after seeing conditions in southern Europe, especially among the peasant class, my ideas regarding my race changed entirely and I realized for the first time that the Negro in America, even the most backward Negro farmer, notwithstanding the unfairness and injustice which confront him, lives amidst surroundings much more encouraging and hopeful than is true of certain classes of the white race in Europe. While there was a striking difference in the physical surroundings and economic opportunities between the southern European peasant and the average Negro tenant farmer or renter, and while I also found a very striking difference in the wage scale which affects food, clothing, and home life in general, much to the advantage of the Southern coloured man, there was another difference even more striking, and that was the fact that the average European, to whom I have referred, was inclined to be hopeless so far as any improvement in his present condition was concerned. Few of them, moreover, had much hope of improvement for their children. They themselves were living much as their forefathers had lived, and in many cases they had lived for generations in the same house and worked on the same land with no other future before them save a desire on the part of a few of the younger ones to go either to North or South America. This was about the only ray of hope they had.

On the contrary, the American Negro generally expects that this year's crop will pay him out of debt and that he will at some time, in all probability, own his farm and house. More than that, he expects that his children will live better than he lives. He looks forward to their becoming educated and owning homes and land and prospering generally. To me the most striking difference, therefore, was a difference in attitude of mind. The firm belief of the coloured man in the ultimate triumph of right and justice constitutes his largest and most valuable asset.

What I have said of conditions in Europe is true to some extent also of the Negro in Jamaica. While there is an absence there of the outward manifestations of racial antagonisms such as frequently obtain in this country, and while the difficulties in Jamaica, according to my observations, are due more largely to differences in character rather than in colour, nevertheless the situation so far as it concerns the Negro is in some particulars very much like that of the peasants of southern Europe.

There is this difference, however, between these countries and our own, and that is that the peasant in Europe and Jamaica has no fear for his life; he need not fear the aggressions of the lawless element of his community. If a crime has been committed he knows that the guilty will be tried by the usual legal process and punished accordingly. He knows also that there is no probability of unoffending persons being oppressed and terrorized by any part of the community because of the alleged misconduct of some member of their social or racial group. However, at the end of this trip I landed on American shores with the feeling that whatever may be the disadvantages and inconveniences of my race in America I would rather be a Negro in the United States than anybody else in any other country in the world. My subsequent experiences abroad have confirmed me in this conviction.

Chapter 8

With North and South

IT IS sometimes thought that schools like Hampton, Fisk, Atlanta, Tuskegee, and others are at a disadvantage because in many instances the heads of these institutions have been obliged to spend a considerable portion of their time in the North raising the funds necessary for carrying forward their work; and I myself have shared this feeling to some extent. It has also seemed to me a matter of deep regret that men like General Armstrong, Doctor Frissell, President Ware, President Bumstead, Doctor Cravath, Doctor Washington, and others, should have been obliged to take a large part of their time and frequently all of their vacations in going from place to place, often with a group of singers, delivering addresses, with a view to creating interest in the work of their institutions. But experience has taught me that, while there are great disadvantages, there are, on the other hand, certain compensating advantages.

I think no other movement has kept the North so well informed on all phases of conditions in the South between Negroes and whites. The kindly attitude of an increasing number of each race toward the other, and the growing desire on the part of the South to see that the Negro is educated, go far toward creating a greater interest on the part of the North in the welfare of the Negro, and a broader sympathy on the part of the people of that section with the efforts which each race is making toward coöperation in those things which make for the development of the South. The heads of these institutions deserve a great deal of credit for the vision and courage displayed in thus interpreting the attitude of the South and the needs of their own work.

General Armstrong used frequently to say, forty years ago, that the North would change its attitude toward the Negro if some strong effort were not put forth to prevent it, and that it was the duty of Hampton, as well as of all institutions interested in the welfare of the country, to bring about a greater sympathy and more helpful understanding between the sections.

It so happened that in almost every year from the time of my graduation at Hampton and even before, I spent some time with the Hampton party in the North—frequently with General Armstrong, and later with Doctor Frissell, usually accompanied by the Hampton quartette—trying primarily to raise money for carrying forward Hampton's work. During that period we visited most of the cities and appeared in many of the leading churches east of the Mississippi River; and while I am not sure of the good that I have been able to accomplish for Hampton or the general cause in this way, I am very sure that the contact with prominent clergymen and laymen, as well as with thousands of less prominent people of the various denominations, gave me a kind of experience and training that is to be had in no other way.

I still recall some experiences I had on one of my early trips with General Armstrong as a member of the quartette and also as one of the "campaign" speakers, helping to raise funds for the Institute.

I had gone the previous spring, while a student in the Senior Class, on a short trip to Baltimore and Washington, but this time we made quite a long tour, going throughout New England and visiting many places, including Boston, which I had always wanted to see. I, with other students, used to argue with Doctor Frissell, who conducted our Current History recitation during my Middle and Senior years, over the relative importance of Virginia and New York, the South and the North, and why the textbooks and the people generally spoke so frequently of the greatness of New York. While I believed what the textbooks said, still I always had a feeling that Virginia was almost as great and important as New York. I argued that while New York was a very important seaport, Norfolk was also a very important seaport; that the Norfolk navy yard was about as great and important as the Brooklyn navy yard. Doctor Frissell never permitted himself to argue with his pupils on this point, apparently lest it should lessen their pride in their own section or state; but I remember how on this trip, one Sunday morning, as we were returning from Brooklyn over the famous Brooklyn Bridge, Doctor Frissell pointed out the elevated railroads in New York, the Post-Office, and many of the tall office buildings, and asked if we had anything like that in Virginia. The point was not lost.

As our meetings during the week were usually held in the evenings, we had the days free, which made it possible for us to spend much time in sightseeing in and around New York. One evening, riding in on the train from Orange, New Jersey, I was telling Doctor Frissell what I had seen during the day, mentioning Central Park, the Zoölogical Gardens, the Metropolitan Museum, the wonderful Palisades, the Egyptian mummies and the great Obelisk, which had only recently been set up. He and General Armstrong asked me many questions about how I liked these things and what I thought of them. The General expressed his great pleasure that I had spent my time so profitably, as also did Doctor Frissell. Doctor Frissell said, with a little twinkle with which those of us who knew him well were familiar, "How do these things compare with Richmond and Norfolk?" I finally admitted that I supposed New York was a greater state than Virginia, and any Virginian knows how hard it is to make that admission; but I still believe Virginia to be a great state, my only concession being that I believe there are other states, North and South, equally as great, with people equally as good.

There were for me many very interesting incidents on this tour. At Troy, New York, General Armstrong was given a banquet by some thirty or forty men of the remaining members of the company that he had recruited in that city when he left Williams College at the outbreak of the Civil War. Their enthusiasm for General Armstrong, who had been their captain, was most impressive. The quartette sang during the dinner and I delivered my little address, after which there were many speeches by these veterans. General Armstrong closed with what was to me a most remarkable and touching speech on the race question, setting forth the duty of the North to the Negro and to the South; the reasons why there should not be any bitterness between the two sections and the races; and what he had observed in the Negro as to his possibilities as a useful American citizen. In fact, this was one of the most impressive addresses I ever heard him deliver.

At Stamford, Connecticut, after our usual meeting in one of the churches, we were all invited with General Armstrong to the home of Dr. John Lord, the historian, where the quartette sang many numbers, and where General Armstrong was asked to make a few remarks. When General Armstrong beckoned for me to come over and I was introduced to Doctor Lord, I became somewhat confused as a lady whispered to me that this was John Lord, the historian. I was familiar with the "Old Roman World" and his "Beacon Lights of History," and I was surprised to find this man, who had actually written books, and such important and interesting ones, to be so simple and unaffected in his ways. He moved about during the entire evening telling stories to one group after another, and spending considerable time with the members of the quartette. I recall that he had a pipe in his mouth. It was sometimes lighted and sometimes not. It was frequently right side up, but I think that it was more frequently upside down. He appeared to be entirely unconscious of himself and took great pleasure in seeing that the Hampton students especially were in no sense neglected. His pleasure and enthusiasm over the singing were most evident. The truth of the matter is that he was so simple and so much like other people that I was almost disappointed.

Frequently, at very important meetings, Doctor Washington spoke for Hampton with Doctor Frissell and myself, and it was interesting that on these occasions he rarely ever referred to his own splendid work at Tuskegee Institute, except to speak of it as a part of Hampton's work.

I have found that usually Northern audiences care little or nothing for oratory or orators as such. A simple, straightforward statement of the situation as we saw it and faced it, and of what Hampton was doing, not for the Negro as a race merely, but for the Negro as a part of the citizenship of America, was the thing that usually was most appealing. I always felt that my own talks were unimportant and ineffective, but Doctor Frissell always insisted upon my going. I thought, and frankly said, in my short talks, that I was there because Doctor Frissell wanted to use me as a sort of sample of the finished product of Hampton.

I remember, however, a large meeting at a Congregational church in Montclair, New Jersey, at which some very distinguished speakers were present, and that I made my talk with considerable nervousness, and was very much surprised, therefore, to read afterward the comment of Dr. Amory H. Bradford, then pastor of the church, which I quote here:

It was my privilege recently at a meeting held in the interest of Hampton Institute to listen to three very able speakers. One was a distinguished doctor of divinity, who has occupied a conspicuous place in the denomination of which he is a member, and who is a genuine orator. He knows how to present his subject as few men do, and that night he was singularly persuasive and eloquent. Another speaker was an eminent business man, who had his material well in hand and who presented it with rare discrimination and ability. When they had finished, one could hardly help the feeling that the black and apparently commonplace coloured man who sat upon the platform would hardly keep the meeting on the high level that it had already attained. He began by apologizing for his presence in the absence of his chief, Doctor Frissell, who was ill, but he had not spoken for many seconds before it was evident that he was a natural master of assemblies. With ease and absolute command of himself, with clearness and with entire absence of self-assertion, he presented his thought on the coloured problem. There may have been abler and more convincing addresses on this subject in other places, but I am ready to bear my testimony to the fact that never here, nor elsewhere, have I heard a more perfect address of its kind than fell from the lips of Major Moton, of Hampton Institute, on that occasion. There was no playing to the galleries, no twisting of facts for effect, no noise, but calmness, moral earnestness, exquisite diction, and a poetical quality that made the speech a gem of its kind. So much has been heard about the impossibility of uplifting the coloured race that one can hardly help asking whether Major Moton may not be an exception. He is no exception. The same may be said of a large number of others.

Doctor Washington also of course saw and appreciated the value and importance of this Northern work. While it took a great deal of energy — and Tuskegee, like other institutions, must have felt the effects of the frequent absence of its principal — yet he realized that the work done in this direction was very much worth while, and believed that "Extension Work in the North" is a "lateral influence" of these Southern institutions for which not only the Negro, but the South as a whole, should be grateful.

Hampton Institute has always been the subject of a certain amount of criticism from some people — not that they objected to Hampton as such — but because they felt that Hampton's emphasis on industrial, or vocational, education and the popularity that Hampton enjoyed in the North and in the South reacted to the disadvantage of institutions that stood for higher education for Negroes. General Armstrong was always conscious that he was never wholly acceptable to the rank and file of coloured people for that reason.

I remember that a very important convention of coloured ministers was held in the town of Hampton and many of the distinguished visitors to the community drove through the grounds. Certain of the more prominent members of the party refused to get out of their carriages. They admired the location and buildings and the general appearance of the campus from the outside, but at a private banquet one evening one distinguished man, in speaking of the community, said that while the Institute physically, from what he could observe, was all that one could wish and that he was glad that the Negroes had the privilege of working on such a campus, as a matter of fact General Armstrong and his corps of workers were teaching the

Negroes to be hewers of wood and drawers of water, and that at bottom he was training the Negro boys and girls to be servants to the white race; that he never saw a more beautiful campus but that it was in his judgment a "literary penitentiary." It was to be expected, therefore, that Doctor Frissell in assuming the principalship of the Institute would have to face, in some degree at least, the same sort of attitude.

After observing this condition for three or four years, I finally came to the conclusion that this opposition to Hampton was due largely to a lack of knowledge of Hampton's methods of work and what was being accomplished by those methods. I felt it would be a good thing if Doctor Frissell and many of our other teachers could see more of the coloured people, and if coloured people could become better acquainted with them; that if there could be a clearer understanding between Hampton's faculty and the coloured men and women with college training, from whom most of this kind of opposition came, it would do much toward removing what seemed to me unwarranted antagonism.

Doctor Frissell readily concurred in the suggestion that we have at Hampton each summer what we hoped would be in a general way an educational conference. This idea, I acknowledge, grew out of the idea of the farmers' conference at Tuskegee, which had been introduced some years before by Doctor Washington, and which had been so successful in helping the Negro farmer in the rural South to do better farming as well as to improve the general life of the community in which he lived. The difference in our situation, however, was that it seemed to us advisable to invite to our conference the educated classes of Negroes, especially teachers and other professional men, along with editors, business men, and successful farmers. At our first conference Doctor Washington presided, after which time it seemed to me and to Doctor Washington also that it would be better that Doctor Frissell, the principal, should preside. To the early conferences we invited no white people, either Northerners or Southerners. The idea was that there should be absolutely free and frank discussion and criticism of Hampton, Tuskegee, Doctor Washington, Doctor Frissell, and any one or anything else that might come up in the course of discussions. Indeed we purposely arranged to have papers on subjects that we knew were under criticism and from men who, as we knew, opposed Hampton methods.

I doubt if up to that time so many Negroes of distinction had ever come together in one assembly as came to some of these conferences. The numbers ran from three and four hundred to a thousand, including, of course, large numbers of school teachers. These people spent from one to three days, as guests of the Institute, seeing and studying the work in trades, agriculture, and other lines at first hand, and at the same time getting something of the atmosphere of Hampton and its work. We had present on these occasions such men as President W. S. Scarborough of Wilberforce University, Dr. Kelly Miller of Howard University, Mrs. Fannie Jackson Coppin, Prof. Hugh M. Brown, President R. R. Wright, Prof. N. B. Young, Prof. C. N. Gresham, Dr. Inman Page, Mrs. Annie J. Cooper, Dr. W. E.B. DuBois, Dr. Francis G. Grimké, Mr. A.H. Grimké, Paul Laurence Dunbar, T. Thomas Fortune, and other prominent educators and leaders of thought among our people.

I do not think that anything that Hampton ever did served more to change the attitude of coloured people toward its work than this movement, which gave them a more intimate knowledge of what Hampton was doing, the type of student developed, and something of what these students accomplished after graduation. It may be said that this was the beginning of Hampton's active extension work. As time went on white people came from North and South, and the discussions went into the various social problems such as health, housing, business, school facilities, and the frank discussion of race relations. The coloured people told how they felt regarding certain matters affecting their relations with white people, and we were able in some ways to get a clearer understanding of the Southern white man's point of view. In all of these discussions, which were always frank and frequently animated, there was never any personal feeling displayed. It had the effect not only of giving the visitors a better knowledge of Hampton, but was equally effective in broadening the knowledge of our workers and students as to the viewpoint of these very intelligent men and women of the Negro race. As a result of these conferences, people came to know Doctor Frissell, and while coloured newspapers frequently criticized many of the white men who were heads of Negro educational institutions, and while it is not improbable that they did not always agree with all of Doctor Frissell's statements regarding the Negro, they rarely if ever criticized him, and for twenty years there was comparatively little public criticism of Hampton Institute.

It was in this period of my life at Hampton, 1905, that I was married to Miss Elizabeth Hunt Harris of Williamsburg, Virginia, who entered heartily into the spirit and life of Hampton Institute. But our happiness suddenly gave place to a great sadness on account of her illness and death after little more than a year.

The extension work of Hampton Institute among coloured people in the South had by this time so developed that it was in need of reorganization. Much had been done by the field workers, under the general direction of the chaplain, Dr. H.B. Turner. Doctor Turner had successively associated with him in this capacity various graduates of Hampton, among whom were Mr. George Brandon, Mr. F. M. Fitch, and at various times Mr. T.C. Walker, a very successful lawyer, partner, and teacher of Gloucester County, Virginia. While these men did very good work among graduates and former students, especially in rural communities—activities which Dr. Wallace Buttrick, of the General Education Board, so aptly called "the lateral influences of Hampton"—there grew out of these summer conferences a more definite organization for working, not only among graduates and former students, but among coloured people generally, especially in Virginia and adjoining states.

At one of these conferences a committee was appointed, of which I was made chairman, to effect a permanent working organization. After several meetings and much discussion we came to the conclusion that Negroes were, along many lines, sufficiently well organized already; if anything, they were over-organized. There were business organizations, diverse farmers' organizations, organizations of professional men, and many religious and social organizations, besides various and sundry secret societies and lodges. As a matter of fact, there are very few coloured people who are not members of some kind of organization, and the secret society to many is almost as sacred as the Church and the Sunday School.

Sometimes people who do not know are inclined to ridicule coloured people because of the many and varied organizations which they maintain, but in this connection they should keep in mind that the Negro is accorded but little share in our Government. But few vote and almost none hold office. He is not even permitted to sweep the streets in many cities, because this is considered a political job, so he organizes his secret societies, shrouded often in mystery—the more mysterious the more popular—and sometimes it is true that he will neglect important duties to go to his lodge; as a consequence of which many people are inclined to become impatient with him. But the employers of these people should keep in mind the fact that in these lodges as well as other organizations they have their officers, their president or "Grand Master," or perhaps "Noble Grand," their secretary or "Worthy Scribe" and other officials; that they have a regular order of procedure and each member has the chance to vote and also to hold office. Parliamentary usage is discussed and followed as far as their knowledge goes. One not familiar with these organizations would be surprised to find how accurate often is the knowledge of Jefferson's and Cushing's manuals and how closely the procedure of Congress is followed in the proceedings of these sometimes very primitive bodies. I dare say that frequently too much time is spent on points of order and other technicalities of procedure, but all of this, we must remember, contributes to the race an important training in the development of social habits and is in effect an effort — crude perhaps and sometimes amusing, but nevertheless earnest — on the part of a cramped people to express themselves in terms of democracy.

In view then of the existence of so many organizations, it seemed an unwise undertaking to start a new organization that had nothing concrete to offer. It would not be a church or a business. It would not "take care of the sick or bury the dead," as was true of secret societies. The idea was to organize Negroes for their own betterment, to combine some of the energy that was going into various things into one movement for the development of the entire community. So it occurred to some of us that it would not be an unwise move to "organize the organizations," which we proceeded to do, and called it "The Negro Organization Society of Virginia." Our object was to experiment in our own state and if it proved to be the success we hoped, it would of its own momentum spread into other states. The motto was: "Better Schools, Better Health, Better Homes, Better Farms." This seemed to be a platform broad enough to take in all organizations of whatever kind or character. A great many organizations as well as individuals accepted the movement with enthusiasm. We elected Prof. J.M. Gandy, of the Virginia Normal and Industrial Institute at Petersburg, executive secretary, with more than the usual quota of vice-presidents and members of the Executive Board. For the first year we proposed a "Clean-up Week" for the entire state of Virginia, and with the endorsement of Governor Mann and the State Board of Health, as well as the State Board of Charities, we launched a health campaign.

I need not mention here that in many places the white people, men and women, as well as the civic authorities throughout the state, coöperated with the coloured people in this movement, giving prizes for the cleanest homes, stables, and backyards, and putting carts and wagons at the disposal of the coloured committees. It was said, when the campaign was over, that Virginia was never so clean in all of its history as on that Saturday night in April, 1913. We had asked every coloured minister in the state to preach a special sermon on Health on the Sabbath preceding, and sent out literature, including circulars and statistics which we ourselves prepared and the State Board of Health published; so that we had not only a clean state, but a very much more intelligent state, especially along lines of sanitation and health.

The next year, as a feature of the same sort of campaigns, we set out to raise three thousand dollars to buy a farm upon which we were given to understand the state would establish a sanitarium for Negro consumptives. We had discovered in Virginia, what was also true of other Southern states, that while there were several sanitaria for the treatment of white consumptives, the only two places in the state where Negroes could be treated for tuberculosis were the state prison at Richmond and the insane asylum at Petersburg; so that a coloured consumptive in order to receive treatment in any institution in Virginia, public or private, had either to be a convict or insane. We used this argument most effectively in our campaign for funds among coloured and white, particularly among whites.

The white people, led by such people as Dr. J.T. Mastin, secretary of the State Board of Charities, and Miss Agnes Randolph, a member of one of Virginia's leading families and secretary of the Anti-tuberculosis Society of the state, were aroused as never before to the appalling need of attention to the situation. It was pointed out that the ratio of coloured to white consumptives was something like three to one, and inasmuch as Negroes cooked the food, washed the clothing, nursed the children, and did the house cleaning for a great many of the white people of the state, the Negro consumptives among them ought to have a chance for treatment, if for no higher reason than to protect the whites themselves. The white people, as well as the coloured, learned their lesson and, led by Miss Randolph and encouraged by Dr. E.G. Williams, chairman of the State Board of Health, the matter was brought before the State Legislature which readily appropriated sufficient money to erect suitable buildings on the farm which had been secured by the Negro Organization Society.

At our first annual meeting in Richmond, Doctor Washington was invited to deliver the principal address, which he did then and continued to do at all subsequent meetings up to his death. He was very much interested in this organization and thought it would be a good thing to nationalize it;

so at the last meeting of the National Negro Business League, over which he presided in Boston a few months before his death, I spoke at his request on nationalizing the Negro Organization Society. I was never, however, enthusiastic about having a national organization, for the reason that I was not sure it had in it all the possibilities that many other people thought it contained.

To our annual meetings people frequently came from other states without invitation, to study its operations with a view to introducing it in their own states. It was gratifying that there were few organizations in Virginia that did not join the movement. Some few ministers, Baptists, felt they could not affiliate their churches with anything except an ecclesiastical organization; but at the same time they put themselves down as coöperating or contributing members and instead of paying the stipulated membership fee of five dollars, they took up a yearly collection for the society, which sometimes amounted to as much as fifty dollars. Since then the Organization Society of Virginia has grown and prospered most successfully with Major Allen Washington, my successor as commandant at Hampton Institute, as president. When I left the state, I could not continue as president of the organization, but have maintained my connection with the movement as honorary president. During the war it proved its usefulness as the organization through which all of the various war movements in the state operated among coloured people—Thrift Stamps, Food Conservation, Liberty Bonds, and all the rest. While this movement in Virginia has done much along the lines of its motto, its most significant accomplishment in my opinion has been the bringing together, as no other movement up to this time had done, of the various elements of the coloured population of the state, such as Methodists, Baptists, Masons, Oddfellows, and scores of other social groups, into a combined effort for the general good.

As Bishop L. J. Coppin of the African Methodist Episcopal Church remarked in one of his conferences regarding the Organization Society: "It is a good thing for any one of my churches to share in a movement that is working, not merely for Methodists or Baptists, but for the highest development of all humanity."

But aside from bringing the coloured people together, what is of equal importance with this is the fact that the Negro Organization Society succeeded in establishing a platform upon which both the white people and the coloured people could work together for the good of all the people. Leading white citizens united with the leaders of our own race, and met frequently to discuss the needs of the situation, such as law enforcement, housing, schools, health conditions, and other topics. White and coloured women discussed the servant-girl problem, the protection of girls in domestic service, the importance of making adequate provision for bathing and sleeping in order to secure reliable help, and many other matters affecting the relations of the two races. I am inclined to the belief that Virginia is probably the best-organized state in the Union so far as race relationships are concerned, and, furthermore I do not think that I claim too much when I say that it is largely due to the effective work of this unique organization.

A short time before the beginning of the Negro Organization Society, some of the leading coloured people in Oklahoma conceived the idea that it would be very helpful if Doctor Washington would make a tour of that state, talking to white and coloured people, with reference primarily to race relationships. At that time racial bitterness in Oklahoma was strong, because the state was rapidly growing very prosperous, the coloured people as well as the white accumulating considerable valuable property, thus making competition in business very keen, and creating more or less racial antagonism. In view of these circumstances certain coloured men of the state arranged this trip, and Doctor Washington invited me among others to accompany him. It happened, however, that I was unfortunately unable to leave Hampton at that time. When I saw Doctor Washington in New York a few weeks after his return from Oklahoma, he was very enthusiastic over the trip, not because of the crowds so much as over the spirit in which they had accepted his very plain advice to both coloured and white citizens.

Because of the success of this trip, a number of prominent coloured men of Mississippi — among them Mr. Charles Banks and Mr. Isaiah T. Montgomery of Mound Bayou, which is a unique Negro town in Mississippi, Mr. E.P. Simmons, Mr. Perry Howard, a leading lawyer of Jackson, and others — arranged for Doctor Washington to make a similar trip through their state. He again invited me and this time I was able to go. It was the most wonderful experience of its kind I had up to that time ever had. Crowds of people met Doctor Washington at every place. We spent a week, beginning at Holly Springs and going to most of the important cities in the state. White and coloured vied with each other to make the trip successful. We had a private car, in which the fifteen or twenty men of Doctor Washington's party rode. We frequently slept in the car at night, especially if we had to make an early morning start to fill some engagement. There were whisperings to the effect that a certain element of white people of Mississippi would not permit Negroes to ride in Pullman cars in that state, but no one took it very seriously. Mr. Banks, who managed the tour, kept in touch everywhere with the authorities, and the railroad officials were continually on the alert. There was not, however, the slightest semblance of trouble anywhere.

At Jackson, a rumour was afloat that our car would be blown up that night after we had gone to bed. Doctor Washington and the rest of us were advised not to remain on the car, and to change our schedule, but some of the city and railroad officials heard of these rumours and without our knowledge saw to it that the car was guarded by private detectives throughout the night. Our first intimation of this came to us from a railroad official the next morning as we were about to leave Jackson for our next appointment. He also told us, what we believed from the first, that there was no foundation whatever for the rumour.

A reference to this trip which appeared in the *Southern Workman* shortly thereafter reflects the impression which was made upon me at that time:

What surprised me most in this experience was that I did not find the coloured people in Mississippi nearly so badly off as I expected. The newspapers give a great deal of space to the bad things. They tell you of the mean things that are sometimes said in Mississippi—that the whites have no business to allow Booker Washington to hold meetings in the state—that Washington is a menace, etc., etc. But you seldom hear from them how ex-governors and mayors, ministers and bishops, professional and business men, Southern white men and women lent their presence at his meetings and expressed their approval of what he said and did.

Mr. Washington stated some very striking truths. Governor Vardaman, and anybody else, may talk, but the white people are not fools and they know that the coloured man has the labour of the South in his own hands and that he needs to be educated and developed, made physically and morally clean for the good of all the country. Said Mr. Washington: "It is often said that the destiny of the Negro is in the hands of the Southern whites. I can tell you that the reverse is also true—the destiny of the Southern white race is largely dependent on the Negro. In every Southern white home the food is prepared by Negro women. Your health, your very life, depends on their knowing how to prepare it. Far more than that—the white youth of the South are being trained in their most tender years by Negro girls. It is of the first importance—to you—that these should be women of clean character." When he told them these plain truths the white people accepted them with applause. He said: "You can't have smallpox in the Negro's home and nowhere else. You need to see that the cabin is clean or disease will invade the mansion. Disease draws no colour line." The white people saw the point when Mr. Washington said these things. and when he told them that the education of the Negro is needed for their sakes as well as for his own, it was without doubt convincing. I have never felt more hopeful and encouraged about my people than I have since my trip through Mississippi.

From that time until his death Doctor Washington continued to make similar trips in other states with the same results. These tours covered Virginia, North Carolina, South Carolina, Florida, Delaware, Tennessee, Texas, and part of Arkansas.

The last trip was made in Louisiana in April of 1915 and Doctor Washington looked forward also to going through Maryland and Georgia. He was kind enough to insist upon my accompanying him on all of these trips. He, of course, was the principal speaker, in fact the only speaker, except in so far as some of us would say a few words at the beginning. He was always pleased to have the large audiences led in singing Negro melodies, which part I usually undertook. I do not think I ever had such a sensation as we experienced at Ocala, Florida, where he was greeted by probably twenty thousand people at the Fair Grounds. Just before Doctor Washington was presented to the audience by Judge W. S. Bullock of Ocala, he asked me to lead them in singing, "In Bright Mansions Above"; and when we were all singing, the white people unconsciously joining in, a woman of an East Indian cast of features, but coal black and wearing a shawl of oriental colours, rose in the audience and with an exceedingly melodious voice sang with great fervour above all the rest, at the same time waving her red shawl with the rhythm of the music. The entire audience, even to dignified judges, began swaying with the motion of this wonderful singing — and everyone sang. As we say in our more primitive churches, everybody was truly "happy." Certainly I never heard such singing in all of my experience. It seemed that everyone was swept along with the emotional current of the moment. I had to stop the singing for fear the swaying of bodies and patting of feet by the thousands of people on the grand stand would break it down, perhaps with injury to many and great loss of life. When Doctor Washington rose to speak it was plainly evident that he was deeply affected. I had heard him deliver hundreds of addresses and had listened to him a score or more times on this trip, but for an hour and a half he held the audience absolutely within his grasp and he kept the same rapt attention that had been inspired by the music from the beginning of his address to the end. He told the coloured people in his very effective way of the duty they owed to their white neighbours as well as to their own race, touching upon the importance of industry, thrift, and morality, as was his custom; and then he turned to the thousand or more white people and told of their duty toward the coloured people, producing such an effect on the audience as is altogether impossible to describe. One white lady in describing his address for a Southern paper said that he spoke with such force and vigour that she thought he might be stricken with apoplexy at any moment, and that his sincerity and earnestness were irresistible, adding that she had never experienced such sensations in all her life. Then she said, "Suppose he had died? What difference would it have made? For he could never hope to deliver a better address, or do it more effectively than he did this one, nor could he ever create a stronger or deeper impression on any audience." For the moment, indeed, he seemed almost transfigured, and the audience with him.

I recall several times in Louisiana when his physical strength had waned considerably and when he was perceptibly losing his energy and vigour that nevertheless the same impressions and emotional sensations were created as those experienced at Ocala; and, except for the absence of the extraordinary excitement produced by the woman leading the singing and waving her shawl, Doctor Washington spoke with as much vigour and with as telling effect upon his audiences.

I am glad I had the rare chance, not only of seeing at first hand the actual conditions among my own race and the relationships existing between the races in these various states in the South, but of being with Doctor Washington for many days at a time in close, intimate, personal contact. I am glad to have had the chance of seeing how he handled delicate situations and his wonderful poise throughout. I had been with him in scores of places in the North where he spoke to Northern audiences, and had been with him in his own home and mine; for I had been married again—this time to Miss Jennie D. Booth, a graduate of Hampton who, for some years previous to our marriage, had been a teacher in the Whittier Training School at Hampton Institute. Often we talked late into the night on Hampton and Tuskegee and the general situation as affecting the Negro, but nothing in all my contact with him impressed me so much as these occasions when he courageously pleaded the cause of human brotherhood in the section of his country to which he had dedicated his life.

One of the greatest privileges of my connection with Hampton was the unusual opportunity that came to me of touching many and varied phases of its work. Having the direct responsibility for the discipline and military instruction of the young men, Negro and Indian; having a share in the admission of students to the Institute, adjusting, as far as my limited ability went, the relations between the school and its coloured constituency; interpreting, to the best of my knowledge, the South to the North and the North to the South; substituting frequently for Doctor Frissell in his absence from his Sunday-School class, composed of Post-graduates and Seniors; and leading and interpreting, as a layman in music, the plantation melodies, or religious folk songs of my people; as well as helping the Institute in its Northern campaigns for funds and its Southern extension work — all of this gave me a training and experience the value of which it is impossible for me to over-estimate.

Chapter 9

From Hampton to Tuskegee

IN 1915 the annual meeting of the Negro Organization Society was held in Petersburg, and Doctor Washington had as usual planned to attend and had promised to deliver the annual address for the occasion. It was a great disappointment to us all to receive a telegram from him stating that his health would not permit him to be present. Doctor Frissell, who was with Doctor Washington in New York, came on to Petersburg and explained how serious his condition was. He was then in St. Luke's Hospital, New York. Ex-Governor William H. Mann of Virginia, with whom Doctor Washington was to have spoken, delivered a strong address, in which he paid high tribute to the distinguished leader of the Negro race, whom, he said, he was glad to place in the column of Virginia's most distinguished sons.

A few days later I received a telegram from Doctor Washington asking me to come to New York on my way to Detroit and Chicago where I was to fill some engagements in the interest of Hampton Institute. I reached New York on Thursday, going directly to the home of Dr. E.P. Roberts, one of our leading physicians who, with his brother, Dr. Charles H. Roberts, a dentist of the city, was a warm personal friend of Doctor Washington as well as myself. Doctor Roberts had accompanied Doctor Washington to the hospital and was well acquainted with his condition. He informed me that the probabilities were that Doctor Washington would not be with us much longer. I communicated with St. Luke's Hospital and Mrs. Washington answered that her husband was anxious to see me. Going immediately to the hospital I found him in bed, but to me he did not seem as ill as I had expected to find him. His mind was as clear as ever and I somehow felt that a few weeks of rest would put him in shape for the performance of his usual duties. On many previous occasions I had seen him in much worse condition apparently than he appeared to be at this time. I recalled, for instance, that at Tampa, Florida, Dr. J.A. Kenney, the resident physician at Tuskegee, and Dr. George C. Hall, one of our prominent surgeons and another close friend of Doctor Washington, spent the entire night with him and it seemed to me, who occupied an adjoining room, that he could not live through the night. The next day, however, we visited the Robert Hungerford School, founded by Mr. R.C. Calhoun, a Tuskegee graduate, in which Doctor Washington and all Tuskegeeans had and still have a pardonable pride; and here, as well as at Lakeland, Florida, he spoke with as much vigour and as effectively as I had ever known him to speak; and that very morning, while waiting for the meeting at Lakeland, we went fishing on a near-by lake, with Doctor Washington the most enthusiastic angler. To all appearances, he was in better condition than those of us who had not been ill. I recall the frequent surprise of Mr. Emmett J. Scott and the two physicians as well as of the rest of us at the apparently excellent condition in which we found Doctor Washington on the days following these sleepless nights.

In our conversation at St. Luke's Hospital, Doctor Washington did not refer to himself, except incidentally. He did discuss Tuskegee in many phases and told me that Mr. Rosenwald was due at Tuskegee that very day and how disappointed he was that he could not be present to welcome him. I recall how warmly he spoke of Mr. Rosenwald's personal kindness to him, and of what he meant to the Negro race, through the Y.M.C.A., and to the rural school building programme which was just then beginning to get under way at Tuskegee Institute.

At his request I called on Mr. William G. Willcox, a member of the Board of Trustees of Tuskegee, to discuss with him some matters touching the affairs of the Institute, and while I expressed my hopes for Doctor Washington's ultimate recovery, Mr. Willcox, knowing of course what the physicians had said, was not hopeful. He discussed with me somewhat the future of the Institute, asking who I thought would be the best man to take up the work in case the worst should happen to Doctor Washington. I mentioned two of the workers at the Institute, of whom I spoke very strongly. He made no reference to me personally. He went into some detail as to what I thought ought to be done in the Institute with its farm, trades, and courses of study. I gave him, of course, an off-hand opinion. He discussed various matters and was quite familiar with the general workings of the Institute. In our conversation Mr. Willcox made mention of no one as a possible successor to Doctor Washington. As for myself, I thought Doctor Washington, if he did not wholly recover, would be sufficiently vigorous to continue the work for many years to come by giving up perhaps some of the more strenuous phases of it. While still in conversation with

Mr. Willcox there was a telephone call from the hospital. Mrs. Washington informed me that Doctor Washington was very anxious to have me come back to the hospital before going to the train that night. I went back and spent the rest of the afternoon with him and Mrs. Washington until train time. He was very solicitous about Doctor Frissell, who at the time was not very well, having already undergone a second operation. Doctor Washington and I knew of Doctor Frissell's condition and I recall Doctor Washington's saying, "What will the race do without Doctor Frissell?" He remarked that Hampton itself would be all right, but he was thinking of the larger work of Hampton, the various phases of life in our country touching the races, which Doctor Frissell so effectively served. I agreed with his suggestion that he should return to Tuskegee as soon as possible. I thought that amid familiar surroundings he would recuperate much more rapidly, as had been true of Doctor Frissell a few months before, when, against the advice of his physician but in response to the wishes of friends, he had gone back to Hampton, which proved to be very wise on his part. Doctor Kenney and Doctor Roberts, as well as the staff physicians of the hospital, held out no hope, but I somehow could not bring myself to believe that the end was so near. This was on Thursday afternoon and I left that evening for Detroit.

On the following Sunday I received a telegram to the effect that Doctor Washington had passed away at Tuskegee. The fact dawned upon me with a peculiar sense of personal loss such as I had never before experienced in the death of any man, not even in the case of my own father. The coloured people generally throughout the entire country had much the same feeling. Observing then as I rode on the train the next day on my way to Tuskegee, I was impressed by the air of depression which pervaded every group. There was a noticeable absence of the usual mirth and lightheartedness generally so characteristic of them. I have never known anything to impress the coloured people so profoundly as did the passing of Doctor Washington. I had often heard that when the word came that President Lincoln had been shot the coloured people went about as if they had lost the dearest member of their immediate family, and that this feeling was largely shared by white people as well, especially the older ones. This same attitude seemed to prevail among the coloured people at the passing of Doctor Washington.

I found on reaching the Institute that it was Mrs. Washington's wish, in keeping with the spirit of Doctor Washington himself, that the funeral service should be very simple, that there should be no addresses or funeral orations, just a simple service, with the singing of plantation melodies and some of his favourite hymns.

As a part of this service, Doctor Frissell, who had been one of Doctor Washington's early teachers, offered prayer. The following passages taken from it reveal its beautiful spirit and touching sympathy:

"Thanks be unto God who giveth us the victory."

We thank Thee for thy servant whom thou hast called home—for his life of faith; that he endured as seeing him who is invisible; that like Thy servant of old he chose to share ill treatment with the people of God rather than enjoy the pleasures of sin for a season; that he counted the reproach of Christ greater riches than the treasures of Egypt; that he looked unto the recompense of the reward.

We thank Thee for the life of love that he lived; that no man, white or black, North or South, could drag him down so low as to make him hate him. And that he taught men everywhere to love one another; that he preached the gospel of peace and good will. We thank Thee for his life of meekness, that his life was one of humility; that he did not think of himself more highly than he ought to think. And we thank Thee for the inheritance that was his because of his meekness. We thank Thee that he did inherit the earth.

We thank Thee for his loving friends, for his devoted coworkers and pupils, for this great school. We thank Thee for his life of service; that he made blind eyes to see; that he, like his Master, made lame men to walk; that he, too, brought liberty to the captives. We thank Thee for the thousands of better homes and farms that he made possible. We thank Thee for the better schools and churches. We thank Thee for the thousands of purer and better lives which he helped to create.

And now we dedicate ourselves anew to the work to which Thy servant gave his life. Help us to realize the high and holy calling that was his and is ours. Help us that we may carry on the work to which he gave his life.

Support us all the day long of this troublous life until the shadows lengthen and the evening comes and the busy world is hushed and the fever of life is over and our work is done. Then in Thy mercy grant us a safe lodging and a holy rest and peace at last with Jesus Christ our Lord, Amen.

Following this prayer, offered by a man whose own days were numbered—as a few of us knew at the time—about a man to whom he had given his entire confidence and for whom he had the most affectionate regard, a former pupil of his, all depression was dispelled and the great audience seemed to get a new vision of what Doctor Washington's life had meant and to feel that its end was indeed a victory.

After the funeral ceremonies the Hampton graduates at Tuskegee, following their usual custom, asked to have Doctor Frissell meet them informally later at the home of one of their number. In the course of the evening Doctor Frissell called me aside and remarked: "It appears you will have to leave Hampton and come to Tuskegee." Now it was in May of the same year that Doctor Frissell, as he was leaving Hampton to go to New York for his second operation, had called me into his office the afternoon before his departure and asked me if I would promise him that I would remain permanently at Hampton Institute. I told him that I would. He had spoken of his own condition, saying that while his health was in better shape, so the doctor said, and he felt better than when he had been operated on two years before, yet he was not sure what the outcome would be and that if I would promise to remain at Hampton, whatever happened, he would feel very happy. Of course, it was not difficult to promise this because it was wholly in keeping with what I had planned. After twenty-six years as a worker I had rather settled down to the life and work there. I was enjoying my work and was especially interested in the development of the extension department in connection with the Negro Organization Society. Doctor Frissell had permitted me to give as much time as I wished to it, and I had taken on an other assistant in my work in the Institute in order that I might devote more of my time to extension activities in both North and South. I reminded him of that promise made a few months before. He said, "Yes, and I am loath to have you break that promise, but it looks now as if you will have to take this work. There will be a great protest at Hampton about your leaving, but you and I will have to face it. Hampton has never refused to give to Tuskegee anything that it had, and if you are asked to take this work, as I am afraid now that you will be, there is nothing else for us to do but consent."

On the 14th of December, 1915 at the request of Mr. Seth Low, chairman, I joined the Trustees' party as they were returning from Tuskegee after their meeting following the memorial exercises and rode with them from Charlotteville to Washington. In the party were Mr. Seth Low, Colonel Roosevelt, Mr. William G. Willcox, Mr. Frank Trumbull, Mr. William M. Scott of Philadelphia, and Mr. Charles E. Mason of Boston. They informed me that my name was under consideration as Doctor Washington's successor at Tuskegee Institute. I told them of my general attitude toward the matter. I told them of Doctor Frissell's condition and of my obligation to him and Hampton. They did not comment on what I had to say but asked a great many questions about various matters affecting Tuskegee. This was especially true of Colonel Roosevelt who the next day sent to one of the Trustees who was not present at the meeting on the train a letter containing the following excerpt describing his own attitude in the situation, a copy of which letter he later sent to me:

We all of us ardently wish you had been with us on the train when we saw Major Moton . . . I am more impressed than I can well express with Major Moton. It is the greatest relief to me to say that I believe that if he is appointed we insure for ourselves every reasonable probability of success in carrying on the great work of Booker T. Washington. I believe that he can run the institution. I believe that he will get on with the Southern people as well as any Negro now living—I bar Booker T. Washington because he was a genius such as does not arise in a generation. I believe that he will get on with Northern white men and be able to help us in getting the necessary funds. He has a very powerful and at the same time an engaging and attractive personality. I cannot speak too strongly about the favourable impression he has made on me. Finally I believe that he will be able to wisely interpret the feelings and desires of his own people to the white people of both the North and the South.

The vice-chairman of the Board of Trustees and president of the Macon County Bank, Mr. W. W. Campbell, who through his father had known and been interested in the school from its beginning, and two other of the local trustees, a prominent lawyer, Mr. C. W. Hare, and a successful coloured merchant, Mr. A. J. Wilborn, as well as others, were particularly anxious that the man who should succeed Doctor Washington should have the right attitude toward both races. During the week of the 13th to the 20th of December, Mr. Campbell, I afterward learned, being a member of the committee of five appointed by the board with power to select a principal, without the knowledge of any one, so far as I know, made a trip to Virginia to find out at first hand what the people of that state thought of the man proposed for the principalship. He visited Danville, Lynchburg, and other places; talked with the president of the University of Virginia and on the streets with many men, white and black; and then proceeded to Richmond and Hampton. He conversed much with the people of Hampton, among them Judge C.W. Robinson, judge of the circuit court, who afterward said that, while he was a truthful man, he was tempted on this particular occasion to tell Mr. Campbell that he did not think I would in any sense do, owing to his reluctance to have me leave Virginia. After he questioned many people in the town of Hampton, Mr. Campbell came over to the Institute to call on Doctor Frissell on Sunday afternoon. He and Doctor Frissell had a conference of perhaps an hour, into which they later invited me. He announced frankly the purpose of his visit but said very little regarding what he had discovered or the impression that had been made upon him. I had been asked to meet the committee the following day in the office of Mr. Frank Trumbull at 71 Broadway. I met the committee, composed of Mr. Seth Low, Mr. Frank Trumbull, Mr. Edgar A. Bancroft, Mr. Campbell, and Mr. V.H. Tulane, the last mentioned a prominent coloured business man of Montgomery, Alabama. At the close of the meeting Mr. Campbell assured me that all he had heard in Virginia was satisfactory.

The outcome of it all was that I was asked to take the work. I knew the difficulties that I would have to face, not only at the Institute itself but in the country generally. I had lived a sort of independent life at Hampton and I felt, of course, that I was accomplishing some good, and while I was in no sense lacking in appreciation of the honour and the opportunity offered by the work of the Tuskegee Institute, I had no particular enthusiasm about giving up the life and work at Hampton. I knew, too, of Doctor Frissell's condition. I knew, as very few knew outside of his immediate family, the character of his malady and that he probably would not live much more than twelve months longer, and while he had released me from my promise, nevertheless I felt a deep obligation both to him and to Hampton. Mrs. Moton—along with many of my intimate friends North and South—shared this feeling very strongly, but after canvassing the situation most carefully, Mrs. Moton and I concluded that there was nothing else for me to do but accept.

To enter upon the varied and delicate responsibilities growing out of Doctor Washington's life work was not to be lightly undertaken, and I confess that I would have had many and even more serious misgivings about many things, in spite of the assurances of Tuskegee's Trustees and of many of my own friends, had it not been for the kind and generous encouragement of Doctor Washington himself, given at a time when neither of us contemplated even remotely any possible significance and value that might attach to his statements as he set them forth in his book, "My Larger Education," from which I quote:

It has been my privilege to come into contact with many different types of people, but I know few men who are so lovable and at the same time so sensible in their nature as Major Moton. He is chock-full of common sense. Further than that, he is a man who, without obtruding himself and without your knowing how he does it, makes you believe in him from the very first time you see him and from your first contact with him, and at the same time makes you love him. He is the kind of man in whose company I always feel like being, never tire of, always want to be around him, or always want to be near him. Although he has little schooling outside of what he was able to get at Hampton Institute, Major Moton is one of the best-read men and one of the most interesting men to talk with I have ever met. Education has not "spoiled" him, as it seems to have done in the case of some other educated Negroes. It has not embittered or narrowed him in his affections. He has not learned to hate or distrust any class of people, and he is just as ready to assist and show kindness to a white man as to a black man, to a Southerner as to a Northerner.

My acquaintance with Major Moton began, as I remember, after he had graduated at Hampton Institute and while he was employed there as a teacher. He had at that time the position that I once occupied in charge of the Indian students. Later he was given the very responsible position of Commandant of Cadets, in which he has charge of the discipline of all the students. In this position he has an opportunity to exert a very direct and personal influence upon the members of the student body and, what is especially important, to prepare them to meet the peculiar difficulties that await them when they go out in the world to begin life for themselves.

It has always seemed to me very fortunate that Hampton Institute should have had in the position which Major Moton occupies a man of such kindly good humour, thorough self control, and sympathetic disposition.

Major Moton knows by intuition Northern white people and Southern white people. I have often heard the remark made that the Southern white man knows more about the Negro in the South than anybody else. I will not stop here to debate that question, but I will add that coloured men like Major Moton know more about the Southern white men than anybody else.

At Hampton Institute, for example, they have white teachers and coloured teachers; they have Southern white people and Northern white people; besides, they have coloured students and Indian students. Major Moton knows how to keep his hands on all these different elements, to see to it that friction is kept down, and that each works in harmony with the other. It is a difficult job, but Major Moton knows how to negotiate it.

This thorough understanding of both races which Major Moton possesses has enabled him to give his students just the sort of practical and helpful advice and counsel that no white man who has not himself faced the peculiar conditions of the Negro could be able to give.

I think it would do anyone good to attend one of Major Moton's Sunday-School classes when he is explaining to his students, in the very practical way which he knows how to use, the mistake of students allowing themselves to be embittered by injustice or degraded by calumny and abuse with which every coloured man must expect to meet at one time or another. Very likely he will follow up what he has to say on this subject by some very apt illustration from his own experience or from that of some of his acquaintances, which will show how much easier and simpler it is to meet prejudice with sympathy and understanding than with hatred; to remember that the man who abuses you because of your race probably hasn't the slightest knowledge of you personally, and, nine times out of ten, if you simply refuse to feel injured by what he says, will feel ashamed of himself later.

I have seen Major Moton in a good many trying situations in which an ordinary man would have lost his head, but I have never seen him when he seemed to feel the least degraded or humiliated. I have learned from Major Moton that one need not belong to a superior race in order to be a gentleman.

It has been through contact with men like Major Moton—clean, wholesome, high-souled gentlemen under black skins—that I have received a kind of education no books could impart. Whatever disadvantages one may suffer from being a part of what is called an "inferior race," a member of such a race has the advantage of not feeling compelled to go through the world, as some members of others races do, proclaiming their superiority from the housetops. There are some people in this world who would feel lonesome, and they are not all of them white people either, if they did not have someone to whom they could claim superiority.

Immediately after my election I was asked by the Trustees of Tuskegee Institute to devote the next few months to helping them raise a fund of

$2,000,000 which they were asking of the public as a memorial to Doctor Washington. I could not undertake the work immediately, because of a number of speaking engagements with Hampton which were to last until the early part of February, at which time I entered actively into the effort of raising the Memorial Fund.

In the meantime, I went down to Tuskegee during the Christmas holidays and remained over New Year's Day looking into things and getting acquainted as far as I could with the situation; for, while I had visited Tuskegee once or twice a year for many years, and had looked into the work many times, it had never occurred to me that I would ever work at Tuskegee, to say nothing of having the responsibility for all its activities. I met the heads of the various departments in an unofficial way, talked over their work and plans, and met and talked with many of the other workers as well as students, trying to get also some knowledge of the character of the work that was being done in the trades and industries as well as in the academic department.

In the interval between then and the 25th of May, the time set for my inauguration, I had frequent conferences with Mr. Seth Low, the chairman of the Board, and could not but observe that he was not very well and that each time I met him he seemed weaker than on my previous visit. On a particular day in April when I dropped in on my way to Boston to see him, he turned to me with some emotion and said he was very sorry that he would not be able to be at Tuskegee for Commencement and the inauguration. "I had looked forward," he said, "with a great deal of pleasure and satisfaction to inducting you into the principalship of Tuskegee Institute." No one was more interested in the work at Tuskegee Institute or more anxious for its future than Mr. Low. I recall how with some feeling he advised me as to many phases of the work and workers. I was surprised that he knew so much about the individual workers, even as to their temperaments. He was leaving that afternoon for Broad Brook Farm, where he thought to spend the summer and regain his health. I never saw him again, though I kept in touch with him by correspondence and through Mrs. Low and Mr. Trumbull more or less regularly during the summer.

Chapter 10

At Tuskegee

MANY friends, and newspapers, too, urged me to make a statement with regard to my future work at Tuskegee Institute. The people generally, especially the Southern people, were anxious to know whether there would be any change in the policies of the Institute. Accordingly, I thought that the inauguration at Tuskegee Institute would be an appropriate occasion to set forth my attitude and views concerning those phases of the work in which the public was most interested. Of course, I realized that the hundreds of interested people who assembled here for the Commencement and inauguration came largely because of their interest in Tuskegee Institute, and because they wanted to see and hear the man who was to succeed Doctor Washington. Mr. Low, the chairman, and Mr. Campbell, the vice-president, were both away because of illness, and Mr. William G. Willcox, a member of the Board, presided in their stead. Among the speakers for the occasion were His Excellency, Governor Charles Henderson of Alabama, Doctor Frissell of Hampton Institute, and President H.T. Kealing of Western University, Quindaro, Kansas, representing the South, the North, and the Negro, and reflecting in their words the kindly interest of the three elements upon whose coöperation the Tuskegee Institute has been built up. My own address, which follows, sets forth what had been frequently and urgently requested of me from many parts of the country:

At a time when racial misunderstandings and sectional strife, resulting from the Civil War and subsequent reconstruction, had reached an acute stage, when well-meaning men were trying to find an adequate method of racial readjustment, a Southern white man, and one who had strong Southern feelings, who saw the great need of the Negro here in Alabama and the South, and who was filled with an earnest desire to help him, wrote to a Northern white man with equally as strong Northern feelings, inquiring if a coloured man could be sent to Tuskegee to begin a work similar in plan and purpose to that which had been started at Hampton—a type of education which was at that time not only woefully misunderstood, but bitterly opposed by many of the leading men of the Negro race.

On that day in July, 1881 when the modest, quiet, unassuming young man, Booker T. Washington, reported with a letter from General Armstrong, his former teacher, and was cordially received and welcomed to this community by Mr. George W. Campbell, then it was that a form of coöperation began, the scope and effectiveness of which were destined to command the respect and admiration, not only of this country, but also of the entire civilized world. Here met the three elements—the North, the South, and the Negro—the three elements that must be taken into account in any genuinely satisfactory adjustment of race relations. It was natural for white men to be considered as important factors in any and all adjustments and problems, whether civic, business, educational, or otherwise. Up to this time the Negro had usually been the problem and not regarded as an element worthy of serious consideration, so far as any first-hand contribution was concerned that he could make toward the solution of any large social question.

These two men, representing the two extremes of sectional sentiment —Mr. Campbell, a former slave owner, the South; and General Armstrong, a former officer in the Federal Army, the North—both broad in sympathy and wise in judgment, and entirely void of any selfish motives, both actuated by a sincere desire to reunite the nation in spirit and purpose, as well as in law and lineage, both patriotic American citizens—these two gentlemen united their forces for the primary object of lifting the burden of ignorance, and all the consequences resulting therefrom, in the South. Mr. Campbell wanted a Negro to undertake the work, and General Armstrong knew of at least one Negro, Booker Washington, who could do the work. These three men, in a united purpose for the common good of humanity, began a coöperation which has been strikingly characteristic of Tuskegee Institute, and a coöperation vitally necessary in the promotion of any successful work for the permanent betterment of the Negro race in our country.

The Tuskegee School, from the very beginning, has had a moral and material support and backing from Mr. Campbell and other white people in this community, without which this institution would have been impossible. No one knew and appreciated this fact more than did Doctor Washington, and no one could have been more grateful than he was for it. There were also coloured men who stood by the founder of Tuskegee Institute in those early days. In his autobiography, "Up From Slavery," Doctor Washington fittingly says:

"In the midst of all the difficulties which I encountered in getting the little school started, and since then through a period of nineteen years, there are two men among all the many friends of the school in Tuskegee upon whom I have depended constantly for advice and guidance; and the success of the undertaking is largely due to these men, from whom I have never sought anything in vain. I mention them simply as types. One is a white man and an ex-slaveholder, Mr. George W. Campbell; the other is a black man and an ex-slave, Mr. Lewis Adams. I do not know two men whose advice and judgment I would feel more like following in anything that concerns the life and development of the school than that of these two men."

Needless to say, Mr. Wright W. Campbell has stood by Doctor Washington and the school with the same devotion and sacrifice as did his noble father. I might mention also such men as Mr. Hare and scores of the other white and coloured people in this county and state who were also very kind, sympathetic, and generous in those early days of the school, and I am glad to state that they are equally as sympathetic today.

The experimental seed of this new coöperation which was planted in 1881 by Mr. Campbell, and which during thirty-four years was so wisely, patiently, and devotedly nurtured by Doctor Washington, has grown into a substantial reality in successful racial coöperation and helpfulness here at Tuskegee. It has far exceeded the most sanguine expectations of our most hopeful friends of fifty years ago.

This unselfish working together of the white and coloured races was truly of very great importance, but it was of equal importance to prove what was at that time very seriously doubted—whether there could be developed within the Negro race any forceful, unemotional, business-like, harmonious working together. This was a mooted question, and one about which there was much real, though often kindly and sympathetic, skepticism even among our own people. Doctor Washington, believing as he always did, in the possibilities of this race, set out to prove that Negroes could work together and under Negro leadership, too, in educational as well as in business organizations. The success which those who compose the membership of the National Negro Business League, as well as many others outside the League, have had, was to him a reward of genuine satisfaction for his unfaltering faith in his people.

While he always sought the advice, criticism, and help of the white race, he drew the "colour line" when it came to the actual work of the institution. How well he succeeded is too evident for comment. These grounds and buildings, the consecrated lives and work of the men and women whom he gathered about him, are eloquent and convincing evidence of the wisdom of his course. I think now of such workers as Mr. Lewis Adams, Mr. R.H. Hamilton, and Mrs. Adela H. Logan, who, like our great leader, "have conquered in the fight." We have with us still such faithful workers as Mr. Warren Logan, Mr. John H. Washington, and Mr. C.W. Greene, who were willing with Doctor Washington to bear the "burden and heat" of those early days—these, with many others of the pioneer, as well as the present-day workers, because of their services and sacrifice, have made possible the Tuskegee Institute of today, not merely the grounds and buildings, not even this splendid body of students, but transcendingly more significant and beautiful, they gave us the "Tuskegee Spirit"—the spirit of coöperation and consecration.

That spirit was not and it could not be confined to this campus. It is equally manifest in the lives and work of the thousands of graduates and former students of the Institute such as Mr. William J. Edwards, Mr. W. H. Holtzclaw, Mr. Edgar A. Long, and Miss Cornelia Bowen, who are but types of hundreds of others. They, like our great teacher, are working earnestly to bring about a clearer and better understanding between the races, "hastening that far-off divine event toward which the whole creation moves."

Doctor Washington's ideas of education appeared so simple, so unconventional, and even so unacademic, so vastly different from what had previously been expected of an educational institution, that he was often misunderstood. His methods and motives were candidly questioned in some quarters by some honest people, especially by members of his own race. This feeling took such form as would have discouraged and hampered an ordinary man, but with Doctor Washington, who was truly a prophet and a seer, such opposition served only as a spur to greater and more persistent efforts.

When it was said that he did not approve of higher education for the Negro, he was at that time giving employment here to more Negroes with college training than any other single institution in the land. The fact that he was a trustee of both Howard and Fisk Universities shows that he was in accord with such work. Education was to him the means only, and not the end. The end was life—the life of the ignorant, poverty-stricken Negro who was earnestly longing for a chance. Doctor Washington cared little about the kind of education the Negro received, but he was exceedingly anxious that it should be thorough and well-suited to his reasonably immediate needs. The truth is, the need of industry and skill, of honesty and efficiency, the lack of land and decent homes, the imperative necessity for better methods of farming, together with a woeful lack of morality, which was prevalent among many of the untrained millions of Negroes—all this made such a strong appeal that any system of education which did not offer immediate relief for these masses made comparatively little impression on him.

Doctor Washington worked out a plan of education which showed that the training of the hand should strengthen and supplement the mental and moral activities, especially of those who were fitting themselves for leadership. This system of all-round education for larger service, which was so effectively carried on under his direction, has been so productive of good results that it has attracted the attention and respect of educators the world over. He worked out here a system of correlation of work and study, of industrial and academic instruction, as complete and as satisfactory as could probably be found anywhere. Important and satisfactory as this system was, however, the spirit back of it was of infinitely greater importance. It was the spirit of coöperation between the coloured workers in the school and the white citizens outside of the school, and a consecration for the relief of mankind everywhere, whether in Macon County, the State of Alabama, or in the Nation.

No greater or more serious responsibility was ever placed upon the Negro than is left us here at Tuskeegee. The importance of the work and the gravity of the duty that has been assigned the principal, the officers, and the teachers in forwarding this work cannot be overestimated. But along with the responsibility and difficulties we have a rare opportunity, one almost to be envied—an opportunity to help in the solution of a great problem, the human problem of race, not merely changing the mode of life and the ideals of a race but of almost equal importance, changing the ideas of other races regarding that race. Let us keep in mind the fact that while the outlook was never more hopeful, the Negro problem is not yet solved. True, there are many people who thoroughly believe in Negro education, but we must remember that there are also many honest, sincere white people who are still doubtful as to the wisdom of educating the coloured man. We can and we must convince that class of people that Negro education from every point of view is worth while. While there is great encouragement in the fact that 70 per cent of the Negro population can read and write, it is not safe to assume that 70 per cent of the Negro race are really and truly educated. Our progress in this country has been wonderful, and we have every reason for rejoicing; but ignorance, shiftlessness, disease, inefficiency, and crime are still prevalent among our people. Colour and conduct still count in this question, but let us remember, friends, that conduct counts a great deal more than colour.

General Armstrong, Doctor Washington, and Doctor Frissell, with the support and influence of such Southern men as Mr. Campbell, have shown us the way out, have shown us how these perplexing questions may be met and solved. If we follow the course mapped out here, we shall have the hearty coöperation and support of as distinguished, as wise, as unselfish, and as devoted a body of men as is to be found anywhere in this land. I refer to the Board of Trustees of this institution. Not only so, but we will have also the cordial help and sympathy of the white and coloured people of this state, from His Excellency, Governor Henderson, and Superintendent Feagin, both of whom honour this occasion by their presence, down to the humblest citizen. This whole country, too, will stand by us, if we are wise, sincere, and unselfish. I repeat, our responsibility is tremendous, and our opportunity is great. We should measure up to our responsibilities and our opportunities, and we can do it. Not by arrogant self-seeking; not by bluff, sham, or bombast; not by flippant fault-finding; not by shrinking at difficulty, or shirking duty; not by the cherishing of prejudice against white men or black men can the Tuskegee Institute live and prosper and serve.

In order that this institution shall continue to carry forward the ideals of its great founder, in order that it shall not cease to render large service to humankind, in order that we shall keep the respect and confidence of the people of this land, we must, first, every one of us—principal, officers, teachers, graduates, and students—use every opportunity and strive in every reasonable way to develop and strengthen between white and black people, North and South, that unselfish coöperation which has characterized the Tuskegee Institute from its beginning. Second, we must patiently and persistently and in the spirit of unselfish devotion, follow the methods of education which in this school have been so distinctive, so unique, and so helpful. Third, we must consecrate and reconsecrate our lives to this work as instruments in God's hands for the training of black men and women for service, in whatever capacity, or in whatever locality they may find a human need. Fourth, there must be no cantankerousness here—we must all work absolutely together.

In his last talk from this platform, Doctor Washington spoke on the value and importance of team-work. He urged that officers, teachers, and students, in every department and in every phase of the work, should cultivate, more than ever before, team-work, emphasizing the necessity of this vital essential of the school's success. If team-work, my friends, was necessary in this school under the leadership of Doctor Washington, how much more imperative the necessity is now, inasmuch as we have not the help and inspiration of his strong words and visible presence.

If we are to be true to this great and sacred trust; if we are to carry out the aims and purposes of Booker T. Washington, the founder of this institution, we must each cherish and maintain the spirit which has always permeated the life and work of this place—the spirit of self-forgetfulness—the spirit of service and sacrifice—the *"Tuskegee Spirit"—the spirit of coöperation and of consecration.* It is only in this spirit that the Tuskegee Normal and Industrial Institute can continue to render service to our people, to our state, to our country.

I cannot more fittingly or forcibly close these remarks than with the use of the following words from Doctor Washington's last Sunday evening talk: "We want to have team-work," he said, "not only in the direction to which I have referred, but most of all, highest of all, we want to have team-work in our spiritual life, in our religious life, in the prayer meetings, in the preaching service, in every devotional exercise. We can get it by each one forgetting his own personal ambitions, forgetting selfishness, forgetting all that stands in the way of perfect team-work."

I was very pleasantly impressed on this occasion by the deep and sympathetic interest of the alumni of the Institute, which was indicated by the presence of groups representing various classes which came from many sections of the country. I recall among others a special party from Chicago headed by Mr. Claude A. Barnett of the class of 1906 which brought, besides many alumni from that city, a large number of distinguished coloured people from the Northwest. It was also gratifying to have present on this occasion a large party from Virginia, composed largely of men and women with whom I had been associated for many years in various movements affecting the life and interests of the coloured people of that state. I was very much surprised when, in the midst of the exercises, President John

M. Gandy of Petersburg, in behalf of the group, presented me with a loving cup in token of their good wishes and esteem.

It was reassuring to receive in connection with this event various letters and telegrams from men and women in the South, both white and coloured, who gave me assurance of good will toward the work of Tuskegee and cordial coöperation and support of my own efforts in connection therewith. His Excellency, Governor Charles Henderson, was especially cordial in his welcome to the State of Alabama and pledged his support and the continued interest of the white and coloured people of the state in the work being carried on at Tuskegee Institute.

We have followed closely the policies of Doctor Washington. There have of necessity been some changes and some reorganization. This was to be expected, but there have been fewer changes than might have been expected under the circumstances. Doctor Washington was a man unique in method as well as personality. I had supposed that any one succeeding him would find it necessary to devise plans and methods better adapted to his own capacities and temperament. The fact is, I soon found that he had constructed a working organization that was remarkably simple and equally effective in its operations, an organization that sometimes seemed to function as well in the absence of the principal as when he was present. It was this, in fact, that enabled Doctor Washington and enables the present principal to spend a considerable part of his time away from the Institute in securing the funds necessary to carry on the work.

Among the first to greet me at the Institute was Mr. J.H. Washington, the brother of Doctor Washington and for many years General Superintendent of Industries, who has had a great deal to do with the physical development of the Institute in all of its phases. He joined his brother a few years after the work began and has ever since given himself unreservedly to the interests of the Institute. The confidence and devotion of the two brothers was touchingly beautiful. He has recently been obliged to give up active responsibility, but is nevertheless just as much interested in every aspect of the Institute's work. It is a pleasure and benediction for teachers and students to see him about the grounds, and his advice and counsel are still found very valuable on many matters touching the interests of the Institute.

During the interval between Doctor Washington's death and the inauguration of the new principal the responsibilities of this post devolved upon the vice-principal and treasurer, Mr. Warren Logan. Mr. Logan came to the Institute at Mr. Washington's invitation two years after Mr. Washington himself came. He, like Mr. J.H. Washington, was a graduate of Hampton Institute. Mr. Logan had been teaching school in Maryland. He had not been at the Institute long before the acute financial needs which Mr. Washington continually faced in the early years of the school led him to ask Mr. Logan if he had any money. Mr. Logan answered that he had seventy-five dollars, and seventy-five dollars was a great deal in those days in the hands of a coloured school teacher. It represented, I think, Mr. Logan's savings for two years. Doctor Washington forthwith borrowed it and put it into the work of the Institute. Mr. Logan through all these years has stood by the school with the same spirit of self-sacrifice and, as treasurer, has husbanded its finances in every possible way. Doctor Washington once mentioned to Doctor Frissell and myself that Tuskegee would not have been possible had he not had the help of Mr. Logan. He has held about every position in the school: treasurer, business manager, director of the Academic Department, and almost from the beginning has acted as principal in Doctor Washington's absence. During the interim when he served as acting principal the school went on with its accustomed smoothness. The casual observer would scarcely have known that Doctor Washington himself was not living and present.

Long before the death of Doctor Washington I had known of the great service of Mrs. Washington to the Institute as Dean of Women, which began many years before she became Mrs. Washington. She has been a tremendous force in the development of the school, sharing without reserve the many and increasing burdens which the rapid growth of the school made necessary. While her special work has been the direction of girls' industries at Dorothy Hall, she has been no less active and helpful in all of the other workings of the organization. She has stood by the work since her husband's death as she had done before, with a loyalty and devotion to the best interests of Tuskegee that have known no abatement.

In assuming the duties of principal, I very naturally came into close and intimate contact with Mr. Emmett J. Scott, who for many years served as private secretary to Doctor Washington and later as secretary of the institution. I found him to be a rarely competent and painstaking executive. No one at the Institute knew more about the varied and peculiar activities which Tuskegee fostered outside of the school proper, or sensed more clearly what Tuskegee's attitude should be touching public questions generally.

It was with the help of Mr. Scott that Doctor Washington was able to build up the very effective executive machinery of the Institute and to develop his wide field of public activity.

In the various other departments of the Institute, I found that Doctor Washington had gathered about him men each of whom had a clear and firm grasp on his own particular branch of the work. In the department of Mechanical Industries Mr. Robert R. Taylor was carrying forward his work with admirable efficiency. Prof. George W. Carver in agricultural research and experimental work was accomplishing results that were attracting attention throughout the South and in other parts of the world. The Institute hospital, in charge of Dr. John A. Kenney, I found to be one of the most useful and efficient departments of the work. The department of Accounting in charge of Mr. Charles H. Gibson, and the Boys' Department with Major Julius B. Ramsey as commandant, were, along with others, under the direction of very capable men, all of whom were most loyal to Doctor Washington and coöperated very heartily with the incoming principal.

I know of no educational institution whose Board of Trustees takes a more active and personal interest in its work than is true of the Trustees of Tuskegee Institute. An institution is truly fortunate when men of the type of Mr. William G. Willcox—formerly chairman of the Board of Education of New York City and representing large business interests there — are willing to give so much of their time and thought to the internal affairs of a school like Tuskegee. It was soon after my own coming to Tuskegee that Mr. Willcox consented to accept the chairmanship of the Board of Trustees, following the death of Mr. Seth Low.

Among those associated with Mr. Willcox on the Board of Trustees are such men as Mr. Frank Trumbull, chairman of the Board of Directors of the Chesapeake and Ohio as well as several other railroads; Mr. Julius Rosenwald, president of Sears, Roebuck & Company, Chicago; Dr. William Jay Schieffelin of New York; Mr. Charles E. Mason of Boston; and Mr. William M. Scott of Philadelphia. These gentlemen have been untiring in their efforts to sustain the work of the Institute and have responded to every call upon their time and energy which the principal has made upon them. Not only these men but the wives of many of them have been equally interested and responsive to the needs of Tuskegee. We owe the John A. Andrew Memorial Hospital to Mrs. Charles E. Mason; and much of the equipment for the girls' industries, as well as for their dormitories, to the thoughtful interest of Mrs. William G. Willcox and Mrs. Julius Rosenwald. In many ways these ladies have manifested a keen and discriminating interest in all the activities for girls at the Institute that has been most helpful to their proper development. This is true also of Mrs. Seth Low, who, during the time when her husband was chairman of the Board of Trustees, accompanied him on his visits to the Institute and concerned herself personally about the health and comfort of the girls.

Of course, it was not easy to give up a life and environment in which one had spent more than twenty-five years under very pleasant circumstances. It meant the severance of very close and intimate ties and the giving up of a work not only within but also without Hampton Institute that had taken a very strong hold upon my sympathies and to which I was giving my best thought and endeavour.

Mrs. Moton felt the change quite as keenly as I did and in some ways was more reluctant about severing our connection with the work of Hampton Institute than I was. It was a source of satisfaction to both of us at Hampton to be near our parents, who are well advanced in years. Between my own mother and myself there has always been a real companionship such as has not developed between her and the other children, which was due in all probability to the fact that for some years, both prior to and after my father's death and until she married again, many of the responsibilities of the household, notwithstanding my youth, I was obliged to share. There are seven of us—four boys and three girls. Three besides myself attended school at Hampton and all are married and succeeding in a way that is very pleasing to my mother. One of them, Joshua E. Blanton, is in educational work at Penn School in South Carolina, where he holds a responsible position in a unique institution. My mother even now exerts a very strong influence over all of her children, and any one of them would hesitate to follow a course of which she had expressed disapproval.

Following the inauguration Mrs. Moton and I took up life at Tuskegee in very much the same way that we had lived at Hampton. We established our home amid very pleasant surroundings where Mrs. Moton and our four children—two girls and two boys—have grown to be just as happy and contented as they were at Hampton. While the two institutions are very much alike, there are some aspects in which they are quite unlike. At Tuskegee we have the unique situation of a large institution—really a community—of about three thousand coloured people conducting and directing all of the activities incident to their daily life. While there have always been the pleasantest relations with the white people of the town of Tuskegee and the county as well, the school community is as separate and distinct in its daily activities as if they were many miles apart. Visitors to the Institute, white as well as coloured, generally find it a matter of interest and pride to observe here a well-ordered institution entirely and successfully directed by Negroes.

It was just after the close of this first year's work that Tuskegee sustained one of its greatest losses in the death of Doctor Frissell, the one man, excepting Doctor Washington himself, who in the last thirty years has been most active and helpful in Negro education. There was scarcely a man in the country more genuinely loved and respected by people of both sections and races than Doctor Frissell. For thirty-seven years he was a worker at Hampton, first as chaplain and vice principal, and after General Armstrong's death, in 1893, as principal. Under his quiet, unassuming leadership, Hampton Institute grew, not only physically, but in influence and power among blacks and whites throughout the land. He stood shoulder to shoulder with Doctor Washington in all movements touching the best interests of the South. There was never between the two any semblance of misunderstanding or rivalry. Doctor Washington was always glad, by word or deed, to serve Hampton; and Doctor' Frissell gladly used every opportunity to do the same for Tuskegee. But it is better to let these two friends, one white, one black, each express in his own words his affectionate regard for the other:

His was a wonderful life of faith. I believe that no man without a belief in an overruling Providence could ever have stood what Booker T. Washington stood; could ever have endured what he endured. He believed that down underneath what sometimes seemed like prejudice there was a heart of love, and he found that heart.
— H.B. FRISSELL.

Doctor Frissell is one of the rarest human souls that any one can know. He gives himself—body, mind, and soul—to the service of others. I have never met a man of such rare unselfishness and such rare modesty.
— B.T. WASHINGTON.

Almost the last words of Doctor Washington to me in a New York hospital, three days before his death, were about Doctor Frissell's health, when he expressed the hope that Doctor Frissell might be spared for many years to our race and country. It is hard for one not intimately associated with the two men to appreciate the real love and genuine affection existing between them. They both worked and sacrificed with one unselfish purpose, and for one absorbing and inspiring cause, the bringing to pass of the Kingdom of God on earth.

Mr. Frank Trumbull, in an address at Tuskegee Institute, referred to Mr. Ogden, Mr. Low, Doctor Washington, and Doctor Frissell as "a very remarkable quartette." It was truly a remarkable group; courageous, unselfish soldiers they were; simply, patiently, wisely, unselfishly fighting for broader sympathy and more thorough understanding between men of all races.

After careful and painstaking search Dr. James E. Gregg, of Pittsfield, Massachusetts, was called to be the principal of Hampton Institute; and the Trustees have been most fortunate in finding a man who with great vigour and wisdom has assumed the responsibility of carrying forward that work. Doctor Gregg has manifested at Hampton the spirit so characteristic of his predecessors, which is so much needed in the social and economic readjustments of the nation just now.

Tuskegee and Hampton have always worked in closest sympathy. They cannot do otherwise in the future. The placing of such a man as Doctor Gregg at the head of Hampton and the election of the principal of Tuskegee Institute as a trustee of Hampton will insure equally as great and helpful coöperation between the two schools as in the past, and will also, I hope, help in bringing about greater sympathy and coöperation in all efforts for Negro education.

Chapter 11

War Activities

THE important position which Tuskegee had already acquired through its Founder in matters affecting the interests of coloured people led many persons, officials and others, to turn naturally in this direction for counsel concerning the attitude the Negro would probably assume regarding the war and the best methods to be employed in securing his largest and best service to the nation in the conflict.

The question was early raised as to how he would be affected by German propaganda and whether or not he would fall an easy prey to the schemes of secret enemies of the Government, and allow himself to become an accomplice of spies, plotters, and even bomb-throwers. I promptly assured all questioners that the Negro's loyalty could be depended upon absolutely at this time as in the past. My questioners in many instances pointed out the fact that the Negro had suffered a great many injustices in this country and had long been deprived of many of the rights and privileges enjoyed by other American citizens, in view of which they were very apprehensive lest he should take advantage of this situation and join the enemies of the country in order to avenge his wrongs and secure the rights and opportunities due him as a man and an American. I reminded these anxious people that the Negro in America had always been loyal to his country, even when its acts were sometimes apparently to his disadvantage, and that in this conflict he saw and appreciated the issues at stake as clearly as any other elements in our population.

It has sometimes surprised and even amused me to find white people worrying about the Negro's Americanism, assuming, as they probably do, that because he is black he must have some subconscious and subtle attachment for some other country. They forget that the Negro knows no more about Africa, than these very same white people know about England or some other country from which their ancestors came to America. As a matter of fact, Negroes have been in America practically as long as white people. The Jamestown colonists arrived only thirteen years ahead of them and the Plymouth colony was founded about a year after the Negro arrived. It is not surprising, therefore, that the Negro should be as intense in his Americanism as any other part of our population; and in truth the nation has much less to fear from the approximately twelve millions of her Negro population than from many other groups whose advantages and opportunities would appear to be very much greater, because of a more just attitude which our Government has manifested toward them. It was in this connection that I wrote President Wilson as follows:

> I have not acknowledged your very kind letter of some weeks ago. A number of people of prominence have approached me with reference to the attitude the Negroes would assume in case the country should go to war. I understand also that certain high officials of the Government have raised similar questions.
>
> Notwithstanding the difficulties which my race faces in many parts of this country, some of which I called to your attention in my previous letter, I am writing to assure you that you and the nation can count absolutely on the loyalty of the mass of Negroes of our country; and its people, North and South, as in previous wars, will find the Negro people rallying almost to a man to our flag.
>
> Whatever influence I may have personally, or whatever service I can render in or outside of the Tuskegee Institute, I shall be glad to put at your disposal for the service of our country.

The President replied:

MY DEAR PRINCIPAL MOTON:
Accept my warm thanks for your kind letter of the fifteenth of March and allow me to tell you how deeply I appreciate your generous assurances.

Tuskegee of necessity had to be very active in every line of war work. I felt that there was no better way to show the Tuskegee spirit or to perpetuate the ideals of Doctor Washington than to turn the full force of Tuskegee's resources and influence to the service of our country. The calls came in increasing volume, but no matter what the demands were, whether to give up some worker, to set aside our regular routine, to conduct some sort of campaign, to journey a long distance to address an audience on an urgent war need, or to leave the school on short notice to meet with some committee—we gave freely and gladly of our time and efforts.

When it became apparent that in the application of the draft the Negro would be expected to contribute his full quota of men to the National Army, the question arose as to the desirability and advisability of establishing a camp for the training of Negro officers to command the Negro soldiers, similar to the one that had been previously established at Plattsburg, New York, to which coloured men were not being admitted. The weight of Tuskegee's influence was thrown into this proposal which was being strongly urged from many quarters, with the result that such a camp was authorized by the War Department and was established at Fort Des Moines, Iowa, with Col. C.C. Ballou in command. There was a fear, however, on the part of coloured people that Negro soldiers would be called upon to serve only in what was designated as "service" and "pioneer" regiments—commonly known as labour units—with the possible exception of the comparatively few Negroes who were in the National Guard regiments of several Northern states, and the four regiments of Negro soldiers in the Regular Army. Accordingly, it was urged upon the War Department that to do justice to the Negro it was desirable to have at least one complete Negro division for combat service, officered throughout by coloured men, the hope being that Col. Charles Young would command it. He is at present the only Negro graduate of West Point in the service of the Regular Army, and it should be noted that his record for efficiency is among the best in his grade.

In this connection I was requested to come to Washington for an interview with the Secretary of War. Arriving there I was joined by Mr. George Foster Peabody and together we urged upon the Secretary of War the wholesome effect which such a measure would have in strengthening the confidence of the coloured people throughout the country in the purpose of the Government to be impartial in its attitude toward Negro soldiers. The Secretary was interviewed also by Dr. George W. Cabaniss, and Mr. F. E. de Frantz, and many other coloured and white men of influence. Shortly thereafter the order was issued for the organization of the 92nd Division of the National Army to be composed entirely of Negro soldiers with Negro officers in the line.

It was a great disappointment to coloured people generally, however, that Colonel Young was not given the command of this division, but the War Department, on the advice of the Surgeon General's office, took the position that Colonel Young was physically disqualified for the service. Consequently, the command of this division was given to General Ballou who had been strongly in favour of such a unit.

It was my privilege to visit the various units of Negro soldiers at many of the training camps during the progress of the war. I recall with some satisfaction the two days which I spent with the 1,200 men of the Officers' Training Camp at Fort Des Moines, who for the most part were students from educational institutions and professional men, along with about two hundred men who had been selected from the four Negro regiments of the Regular Army. Tuskegee, like other institutions, furnished its full quota of the men who volunteered for this training camp. Altogether more than forty of our men, teachers, graduates, and students, received commissions at the end of the course and most of them saw service in France. I never saw a finer body of men, and was particularly interested to learn from General Ballou that his surgeon had reported that of the 1,200 men in the group only five had been found on examination to show any signs of social diseases. I doubt if any other camp anywhere could show a better record in this respect than this camp of black men.

Growing out of these and similar experiences it occurred to some of us that, in view of the frequent occasions for conference with governmental officials concerning matters pertaining to coloured people and their part in the successful prosecution of the war, it was highly important to have in Washington, and preferably in the War Department, a wise and capable coloured man who could advise the Secretary in such matters as concerned the relation of Negroes to the various measures set in operation for the winning of the war. It was felt that in this way the Government would secure the fullest coöperation of the coloured people with the least amount of misunderstanding and friction.

In a conference to which I had been invited by Secretary Baker, I made this proposal to him. The Secretary had impressed me as always desirous of being absolutely fair in all his decisions touching the interests of coloured people, and on this occasion it was evident that he was anxious to do anything that would effectively aid in winning the war. After he had gone over the matter quite thoroughly with me, he arranged that I should have an interview with President Wilson. In this interview the President expressed his unqualified approval of the suggestion, and asked who, in my judgment, might acceptably fill such a place, at the same time requesting me to take up the matter in detail with the Secretary of War.

On taking up the matter with Secretary Baker, I proposed Mr. Emmett J. Scott as the man in my opinion who, by his long years of contact and experience with Doctor Washington in the handling of many delicate matters of public interest, was best fitted to advise regarding the many and varied matters which were constantly arising.

Accordingly, Mr. Scott took up the duties of Special Assistant to the Secretary of War, with offices at Washington, the Trustees of the Institute heartily concurring in the arrangement. Thereafter he rendered most valuable service to the Government throughout the war, and while his absence from the Institute hampered considerably the working of his office in the school, we were nevertheless glad to make a sacrifice which contributed so much to the effective service of the coloured people in the war. The school would have suffered very much more, however, but for the very capable way in which the work of the secretary's office was carried forward by Mr. Albon L. Holsey, who, as secretary to the principal, rendered very effective service, not only in the Institute, but in avenues beyond the Institute in connection with various lines of war activity.

While the matter of a representative of the coloured people was under consideration, Government officials were in a quandary over two very important questions; viz., whether Negro draftees should be trained in the South, and whether white and coloured soldiers should be quartered in the same cantonments. It so happened that Dr. P.P. Claxton, U.S. Commissioner of Education, had called a conference of coloured and white men interested in Negro education to meet in Washington and consider various aspects of Negro educational institutions as brought out by the report of the Phelps-Stokes Fund on Negro Schools, prepared by Dr. Thomas Jesse Jones and which at that time had been but recently published by the U.S. Bureau of Education.

It occurred to some of us that it would be wise for Secretary Baker to take advantage of this gathering to get the opinion and judgment of certain of these gentlemen as to the advisable course to pursue with respect to the question of the disposition of coloured draftees in the cantonments. Accordingly, he asked a group of these gentlemen to confer with him regarding the entire situation. Among those present were: Bishop George W. Clinton, Mr. Oswald Garrison Villard, Dr. James H. Dillard, President John Hope, Major Allen Washington, Commissioner T.H. Harris of Louisiana, Mr. George Foster Peabody, and Dr. J.E. Moorland. It was a very illuminating conference. The Secretary asked for a frank expression from almost every individual present, and after some discussion the sentiment of the body was happily expressed bit Mr. Harris, of Louisiana, who told the Secretary of War that he thought the best thing to do was to treat the Negro soldier just as he would treat any other soldier in the United States Army. Put him anywhere, he said, and exact of him the same service, and mete out to him the same penalties for misbehaviour that would be given to any other soldiers. This, in his opinion, was the way to get the best results from black and white soldiers alike and to keep the morale of the country at the highest point of efficiency. While the Secretary did not commit himself, subsequent events showed clearly that this policy was adopted by the War Department and with very satisfactory results.

As the War progressed, the problems of labour throughout the country grew more acute. Here, too, It seemed that the interests of Negroes as well as of the entire country could be best served by having in the Department of Labour an assistant to the Secretary who could serve the department in very much the same way that Mr. Scott was serving the War Department. The National League on Urban Conditions Among Negroes, with which I was connected as an officer, took up the matter, with the result that Dr. George E. Haynes of Fisk University was asked to take up the work with the designation of Director of Negro Economics. This service of the Urban League was only one of the many increasingly helpful measures set in operation by this organization in the interests of Negro advancement. Doctor Haynes himself rendered very valuably service to the Department, as was to be expected; and it was the purpose of Secretary Wilson to continue him in the Department after the war was over, but this was not possible because of the failure of Congress to renew the appropriation for this branch of the service.

At Tuskegee Institute, the demands of the war made serious inroads upon our staff of workers, especially in lines of activity calling for efficient workers in other than military service. In all such cases, we were willing, in spite of inconvenience, to release members of our own force for such work whenever it was apparent that they could be of larger service in connection with war movements outside the Institute.

In the production and conservation of food I felt that Tuskegee should use every possible means to stimulate the coloured people, especially in the South, to their utmost in helping the Government, not only by intensive and extensive methods of farming, but also by putting in a full week's work instead of taking the usual Saturday holiday so common in the rural districts of the South. We were glad, therefore, to release Mr. E.T. Attwell, our business agent, for service with the U.S. Food Administration to direct this campaign among coloured people in the Southern states.

In the same way the Institute later released Mr. Joseph L. Whiting, head of the Division of Education, for educational work overseas with the

Y.M.C.A.; Miss M. E. Saurez, librarian, for service with the same organization in France; the Rev. G. Lake Imes, dean of the Bible Training School, for service with the General War Time Commission of the Churches; and Major J. B. Ramsey, commandant, for War Camp Community Service in Washington.

The very excellent service rendered by Mr. Scott, Doctor Haynes, Mr. Attwell, and other people appointed by the Government, including Dr. C.V. Roman in the Surgeon General's Department, strongly suggests how short-sighted has been the policy of the Government hitherto in not making use of coloured men as a part of governmental machinery, especially in such matters as have to do with coloured people. It is also true, in my opinion, that local government has lost much in efficiency by failing to make use of the service of strong, intelligent coloured men in the local community who could wisely and helpfully assist in the affairs of government among their own people. I have no doubt whatever that crime among Negroes would be reduced at least 50 per cent by the use of Negroes as policemen and deputies where Negroes reside in any considerable numbers.

The Negro press was also found by the Government to be a very helpful factor in the prosecution of the war. It stood almost solidly back of such men as were appointed by the Government in all of their efforts for the country's good. And whatever happened they were most loyal to the Government, even when, as was sometimes true, they might have criticized with justification many of the things which took place. The attitude of these publications, numbering some three hundred or more newspapers and magazines, was a very important factor in determining the attitude of Negroes on many questions growing out of the war; and their influence upon public sentiment among their own people is of growing importance. It is very apparent that white people in the country are taking this fact more largely into account in business affairs as well as in matters of general community welfare.

Very early in the war, the Government selected Tuskegee Institute as one of the institutions to give training along technical lines to certain groups of drafted men who, in contingents of 308 men each, were to be sent here for two months' training. The first contingent arrived on May 15, 1918 and the training of these men continued until October 1 when the last contingent was absorbed into the Student Army Training Corps. In all we trained and issued certificates under Government direction to 1,229 of these men.

Most of them were sent overseas where they were able to aptly apply the technical knowledge received at Tuskegee Institute. We received many letters from these men after they went overseas, telling how the training had helped them.

Along with these direct contributions of men and equipment went the enthusiastic coöperation of the entire Institute community in the work of the Red Cross and the various Liberty Loan and Thrift Stamp drives, as well as loyal adherence to the wishes of the Food Administration.

On the 2nd of December, 1918, at the request of President Wilson and Secretary of War Newton D. Baker, I went to France to look into conditions affecting Negro soldiers, many of whom were undergoing hardships of one kind and another. Secretary Baker said that he and President Wilson felt that my going to France would be encouraging to the men, and that the presence and words of a member of their own race would be particularly helpful, in view of all the circumstances under which they were serving the nation, at the same time inviting me to make any suggestions that might in my judgment help the situation. In spite of pressing matters in connection with the Institute, I felt that it was the school's duty to do anything possible to help our Negro soldiers, and decided to make the trip.

While in France, I visited nearly every point where Negro soldiers were stationed. At most of them I spoke to the men, and at each place I was most cordially welcomed by the officers and men. I also had the privilege of conferring with Col. E. M. House; Bishop Brent, senior chaplain of the American Expeditionary Forces; General Pershing, and many other high officials of the American and French governments, all of whom I consulted with reference to the record which had been made by Negro troops, and received only words of very highest praise and commendation on their character and conduct in all branches of the service.

During the late summer and early fall of 1918, there were a great many rumours, in and outside of official circles in this country, to the effect that, morally, the Negro soldier in France had failed and that the statement that "the Negro is controlled by brutal instincts" was justified. The report was current in France that the "unmentionable crime" was very common; and according to the rumours, Negro officers, as well as privates, in all branches and grades of the service, were guilty of this crime.

A letter I saw that had been written by a lady overseas to another lady in the United States stated that the writer had been told by the colonel of a certain unit, whose guest she was, that he would not feel it safe for her to walk, even with him, through his camp of Negro soldiers. Another letter from a high official in a very important position with the Negro troops overseas, written unofficially to a prominent official on this side, stated that in the And Division alone there had recently been at least thirty cases of the "unmentionable crime."

Another rumour, equally prevalent and damaging, was to the effect that the fighting units which were commanded by Negro officers had been a failure. In other words, "the whispering gallery," which was very active in France on most phases of life overseas, said that the 92nd Division, in which the Negroes of America took special pride, had failed utterly; that, wherever they had been engaged, the Negro officers had gone to pieces; that in some cases the men had to pull themselves together after their officers had shown "the white feather"; and other statements of similar import.

I went to France with authority to go anywhere and get any information from any source, so far as the American Expeditionary Force was concerned. It so happened that I went on the steamer assigned to the newspaper correspondents, a steamer which was one of the convoy ships for the President's party, on which Dr. W. E.B. DuBois, editor of the *Crisis,* was also a passenger. Mr. Lester A. Walton, of the *New York Age;* Mr. Nathan Hunt, of Tuskegee, Together with Doctor DuBois and myself, occupied the same very comfortable stateroom. We had many frank and pleasant talks, both on the ship and in Paris, where we occupied opposite rooms in the same hotel. The subject that we discussed most often was, of course, some phase of the Negro question, always with a view to helping the situation.

I was accompanied on the trips out from Paris, as well as at many interviews in Paris, by two coloured and two white men—one white newspaper man, Mr. Clyde R. Miller, of the Cleveland *Plain-dealer,* and Mr. Lester A. Walton, of the *New York Age.* I also asked to go with me, Dr. Thomas Jesse Jones, of the United States Bureau of Education and the Phelps-Stokes Foundation, and Mr. Nathan Hunt, of Tuskegee Institute.

I realized that the mission was a delicate one, and that questions which I might ask and the things which I would say might probably be misunderstood or misinterpreted. My purpose, however, was to get at the facts and to stop untruthful rumours. In order to ascertain the facts, I made extended inquiries of all those with whom I came in contact. I asked many questions with relation to the conduct and character of the coloured soldiers as compared with other soldiers.

When I reached General Headquarters of the American Expeditionary Force I found that, a few days before my arrival, a young white soldier had been sentenced to be hanged for the "unmentionable crime," but because of his previous good record in every other way the sentence was finally commuted to life imprisonment.

The opinion at General Headquarters was that the crime to which I have referred was no more prevalent among coloured than among white, or any other soldiers.

From Chaumont we went immediately to Marbache, the Headquarters of the 92nd Division. I asked the general then in command of this division about the prevalence of the crime in question. He said that it was very prevalent, and that there had been a great many cases over which he was very much disturbed. This statement was corroborated by conversation with two of his white staff officers, who were present. I courteously asked if he would mind having one of his aides get the records. I said that I thought general statements were often very damaging, and that, inasmuch as the reputation of a race was at stake, I was very anxious to get the facts in order to make an accurate report, and, if possible, to stop the damaging rumours which were becoming more and more prevalent in America and were already prevalent in France, especially among Americans, including military circles, the Young Men's Christian Association, the Red Cross, and other organizations.

When the records were brought in and examined, seven cases where this crime had been charged were found in the entire division of more than twelve thousand. *Of these charged, only two had been found guilty and convicted, and one of the two convictions had been "turned down" at General Headquarters.*

In other fighting units, as well as the units of the Service of Supply at Bordeaux, Saint Nazaire, and Brest, and other places, I made the same investigations. I interviewed American and French commanding officers; I talked, as well, with scores of American and French officials of lower rank. When the records were taken, as with the 92nd Division, the number of cases charged was very few and the number of convictions fewer still. I likewise took much time with certain members of the Peace Conference, and with Americans engaged in various branches of war activity, in an effort to disprove and set at rest this awful slander upon the Negro race. I spared no pains or effort to do this, and it would appear, from subsequent investigations on this side of the water and from reports which have come to me from overseas, that the momentum of these damaging rumours perceptibly lessened.

There was apparently no doubt in anybody's mind in France, so far as I was able to find out among the French or the Americans, as to the excellent qualities of the American Negro as a soldier, when led by white officers. There was also little question about the fighting record of four Negro regiments—the 369th, 370th, 371st and 372nd which had been brigaded with French divisions; but when it came to the 92nd Division, there was a subtle and persistent rumour in Paris and in other places in France, apparently substantiating the rumour which was prevalent in America—only in France it was much more generally accepted as true; namely, that Negro officers "had been practically a failure," and that it was a mistake ever to have attempted to form a division with Negroes as officers.

I took a great deal of pains and care, as did also the gentlemen with me, to run down every rumour. We spent much time in and out of Paris ferreting out every statement that came from the "whispering gallery." We finally found that, so far as the 92nd Division was concerned, only a very small detachment of a single battalion of one regiment had failed.

Later, in talking with General Pershing in France, regarding this story of the failure of Negro officers, he said that the probabilities were that any officers, white or black, under the same adverse circumstances that these men faced, would have failed. A few officers of the battalion were sent before a court martial for trial for having shown cowardice. Not all of them, however, were found guilty. And since then, these cases have been reviewed by the War Department, and the President, on the recommendation of the Secretary of War, has disapproved the proceedings involving the four officers of the 368th Infantry convicted by court martial abroad. After thorough investigation the War Department issued the following statement with regard to this one battalion of the 368th Regiment:

The 368th Regiment had not had battle experience prior to its assignment to the French brigade. It was expected to operate as a liaison organization, maintaining contact with combat forces on either side, but not itself as an attacking force. In the development of the battle it became necessary to use the regiment in attack.

The ground over which the 368th Regiment advanced was extremely difficult. It had been fought over and fortified for four years, and consisted of a dense belt of intricate barbed wire, through which in four years underbrush had grown, concealing the wire and making any advance most difficult. The section in which the regiment was engaged developed at times intense shell, machine-gun, and rifle fire and subjected those troops to a severe test.

The regiment was not fully supplied with wire cutters, maps, and signalling devices. This was in part due to the fact that the troops were serving at the time with the French, from whom the supply was finally received, the delay being caused doubtless by the hurried movement of the regiment and the assumption on the part of the French that it would be supplied from American depots, and on the part of the Americans that it would be supplied by the French, with whom it was serving—a misunderstanding explained only by the confusion and emergencies of battle.

It was gratifying even then to find that the commanding general, who knew all phases of the affair, did not take this failure nearly so seriously as the rumour about it seemed to suggest. The facts in the case in no sense justified the common report.

In talking with the commanding general at Le Mans, I referred to the fact that something like fifteen Negro officers had been sent back as "inefficient." He said to me: "If it is of any comfort to you, I will tell you this: we sent back through Blois to America, in six months, an average of one thousand white officers a month, who failed in one way or another in this awful struggle. I hope, Doctor Moton," he added, "that you won't lose your faith in my race because of this, and certainly I am not going to lose my faith in your race because of the record of a few coloured officers who failed."

We talked with Colonel House, Mr. Ray Stannard Baker, Captain Walter Lippman, leading Y.M.C.A. workers, and many others. All assured me that they were glad to get the facts, and that, so far as they were able, they would stop the slanderous rumours concerning our Negro soldiers. I spoke to white officers in a number of places—at one place to two hundred of them—and candidly stated the facts in the case. I raised the question, if they did not think it was a good and fair thing to stop this rumour of the "whispering gallery," which was defaming a race, which threatened to cut down the efficiency of Negro troops, and was, of course, putting America in a bad light before the world.

Many of the difficulties and troubles among the officers and men of the 92nd Division, as well as other colored units, could have been avoided if we had had at General Headquarters in France a coloured man to render the same wise, dignified, and efficient help as Mr. Emmett J. Scott, secretary of Tuskegee Institute, so splendidly rendered in the War Department at Washington to both the race and the nation. President John Hope, of Morehouse College, Atlanta, Georgia, who under many and trying conditions had done excellent work overseas in connection with the Y.M.C.A., felt this need very much. General Pershing would gladly have had such a man if it had previously occurred to any of us to suggest it.

In almost every instance I found the commanding officers open to suggestions with a view to relieving the needless embarrassment of the coloured soldiers. I found in the Service of Supply that coloured stevedores were working twelve and sixteen hours a day, and sometimes more, which made it impossible for the Y.M.C.A. to do any effective work along educational lines with the thousands of coloured soldiers in this branch of the service. I took this matter up with the commanding general, and within three days orders had been given to reduce the time of work to eight hours. At several places the quarters of the coloured men seemed unfavourably located. In various instances changes were soon made.

I took up with care also, going to the source of the trouble, the matter of excluding coloured women from France. Here, again, I found that there seemed to be no justification for the exclusion of women of our race from overseas service. This I took up with the proper authorities, military and otherwise, and before I left arrangements had been made to send for more of our coloured women, and men also. The best Y.M.C.A. facility I saw, from every point of view, was the one where Mrs. W. A. Hunton, Mrs. J. L. Curtis, and Miss Katharine Johnson were located. There was here a very fine spirit of coöperation between the white and coloured workers. Mr. Wallace, the manager of the district, whom I later met in Paris, was warm in his praise of Secretary Nichols, Secretary Whiting, Chaplain Oveltrea, and other coloured workers.

I took the opportunity wherever it presented itself to speak to our men about the splendid record which they were making and of the danger that would attend any failure on their part to maintain their record untarnished. I said:

"The record you have made in this war, of faithfulness, bravery, and loyalty, has deepened my faith in you as men and as soldiers, as well as in my race and country. You have been tremendously tested. You have suffered hardships and many privations. You have been called upon to make many sacrifices. Your record has sent a thrill of joy and satisfaction to the hearts of millions of black and white Americans, rich and poor, high and low. Black mothers and wives, sweethearts, fathers, and friends have rejoiced with you and with our country in your record.

You will go back to America heroes, as you really are. You will go back as you have carried yourselves over here—in a straightforward, manly, and modest way. If I were you, I would find a job as soon as possible and get to work. To those who have not already done so, I would suggest that you get hold of a piece of land and a home as soon as possible, and marry and settle down... Save your money, and put it into something tangible. I hope no one will do anything in peace to spoil the magnificent record you have made in war."

In the same way I took advantage of many opportunities to speak to white soldiers, officers and men, about their duty to their coloured comrades who were sharing with them the hardships of the war.

I said in my talk:

"These black soldiers, officers and men, have with you willingly and gladly placed their lives at the disposal of their country, not only to make the world safe for democracy, but, of equal importance, to make democracy safe for mankind, black and white. You and they go back to America as heroes, brave and modest, of course, but there is a difference; you go back without let or hindrance with every opportunity our beloved country offers open to you. You are heirs of all the ages. God has never given any race more than he has given to you. The men of my race who return will have many unnecessary hardships and limitations along many lines. What a wonderful opportunity you have, therefore, and what a great responsibility for you, to go back to America resolved that so far as in your power lies you are going to see that these black men and the twelve millions of people whom they represent in our great country, who have stood so loyally by you and America in peace and in war, shall have a fair and absolutely equal chance with every other American citizen, along every line. This is your sacred obligation and duty. They ask only fair play and, as loyal American citizens, they should have it. "

I cannot conclude without again mentioning the heroic record of all of our men in France, especially the Negro officers, who, in spite of hardships and discrimination from sources which should have accorded them much encouragement, went into battle with dash, courage, and an absolutely unshaken and undisturbed morale. I do not believe that men of any other race, under similarly trying circumstances, could have retained more self-possession and made a more glorious record than did our Negro soldiers, officers and men. I am glad that most of those from Tuskegee Institute have returned and taken up their work as before. We cherish, however, the memory of Lieut. Henry H. Boger, one of our teachers, who, with many other brave Americans, sleeps beneath the sacred soil of France.

Before leaving France for London, President Wilson sent me the following letter:

Paris, January 1, 1919.
DEAR PRINCIPAL MOTON:
I wish to express my appreciation for the service you have rendered during the past few weeks in connection with our coloured soldiers here in France. I have heard, not only of the wholesome advice you have given them regarding their conduct during the time they will remain in France but also of your advice as to how they should conduct themselves when they return to our own shores. I very much hope, as you have advised, that no one of them may do anything to spoil the splendid record that they, with the rest of our American forces, have made.

Cordially and sincerely yours,
WOODROW WILSON.

Chapter 11

Forward Movements in the South

THE years since the Civil War have seen the race problem come to the point where it may be discussed without the passion and prejudice which for so many years were characteristic of many who essayed to deal with it. I recall an experience of mine of some twenty years ago when a prominent Southern clergyman dropped into my office at Hampton Institute one evening, and we fell into a rather frank and somewhat heated discussion of certain phases of the race question. At the end of something like an hour and a half of earnest conversation, it was apparent, as was to be expected, that we did not wholly agree upon some aspects of the question; but as we parted he turned to me and said, "Major Moton, our conversation may have struck you as rather unpleasant in some of its features, but for fear that it may discourage you in your efforts to promote harmony between your race and mine, I want to say that I think we are both to be congratulated on the fact that I have reached the point where it is possible for me to discuss this question with you, or with any other coloured man." There are a great many such people in the South today, and this attitude has become much more general than most people who do not come in touch with the situation realize.

Many forces have been operating more or less quietly, but none the less effectively, to bring about this change of attitude toward this one-time delicate and embarrassing problem. For there was a time when most Southern white men felt that there was nothing about the question of the Negro to discuss with anybody, and especially with persons, white or black, whose opinions were likely to differ from their own.

For a great many years I entertained the idea that while the Southern man thought logically and clearly on economic, political, religious, and other questions affecting the welfare and progress of the country, here was one question upon which he did not *think* at all, but rather *felt*—that on this matter he had definite, fixed opinions about which argument was unnecessary and upon which nothing further could be said. But no one can justly entertain that idea about Southern white men as a whole today. While they still *feel* strongly on many points concerning the relations of the two races, there are increasingly large numbers in all parts of the South who are *thinking*, both logically and seriously, on all points touching race relationships, with a sincere desire to bring about such a happy and wholesome adjustment as will be fair and just to both races.

On the other hand, it was true at one time that the great majority of coloured people had very little confidence in the ability or even the desire of the average Southern white man to approach this question without bias, and in consequence looked with suspicion upon any profession of friendliness or good will toward the black man that came from that source. Doctor Washington in his early career was frequently criticized by members of his own race for his freely expressed confidence in the genuineness of the Southern white man's friendship for the Negro. But in late years the Negro's confidence in his white neighbour here in the South has grown to the point where he is turning more naturally to the Southern white man in the confident hope that together they will work out without prejudice or suspicion the great human problems that confront them. Throughout the South the coloured people are bringing directly and officially to the attention of the public the palpably inadequate provisions for the education of their children, and are meeting with an increasingly sympathetic and encouraging response both from the state and from private citizens.

This change in attitude on the part of both races has come about not through indifference and neglect and the proverbial working of time, but as a result of certain carefully thought-out and deliberately planned movements in which Northern white men, Southern white men, and Negroes have wisely and bravely coöperated—movements which I have sometimes felt have been very much misunderstood and the value of whose service to the South and to the nation has been greatly underestimated.

Among the first of these was the Conference for Education in the South, inaugurated by a few men, Northerners and Southerners, who met in a little hotel in the mountains of West Virginia, which conference was presided over by the Hon. William L. Wilson of tariff fame and at one time president of Washington and Lee University. This conference emphasized the necessity of educating all the children of the South.

In the years that followed, this movement brought together such men as Mr. Robert C. Ogden, who became one of America's great educational statesmen; Mr. William H. Baldwin, Jr., who here received the inspiration for the General Education Board, of which he was the first chairman; Mr. John D. Rockefeller, Jr., who, with his father, liberally supported the movement in its development; Mr. Edgar Gardner Murphy of Alabama, secretary of the conference until his death; President Edwin Alderman of the University of Virginia; Mr. George Foster Peabody of New York; Dr. J.D. Eggleston, now president of Hampden Sydney College of Virginia; Dr. H. B. Frissell of Hampton Institute; Mrs. B.B. Munford, one of Virginia's most distinguished women; Dr. Walter H. Page, late ambassador of America to Great Britain, a genuine and unaffected American; and Dr. Wallace Buttrick, for many years secretary and now president of the General Education Board.

I doubt if any movement in America has accomplished more in creating sentiment or has so strongly affected public appropriations for education. As a result of this movement one state alone erected in the neighbourhood of seventy high schools in a single year, while in a few years appropriations for education in Southern states were increased by more than sixteen million dollars.

There is also a close and intimate connection between this conference and the establishment of the General Education Board, which, in supporting the farm-demonstration movement, introduced by Dr. Seaman A. Knapp, and in its present programme of providing supervisors for rural schools in coöperation with state and county boards of education in the South, and making direct appropriations to selected educational institutions, is sowing the seed of educational and economic advancement in the field which was prepared by the labours of this group of distinguished and public-spirited men and women who constituted the Conference for Education in the South, The very substantial service which the General Education Board is rendering will become increasingly apparent in the coming years.

Another force that has been very effective in bringing about a better understanding and a greater measure of confidence between the races is the Negro Rural School Fund: Anna T. Jeanes Foundation. This organization is unique in the fact that on its official Board Negroes, Northern white men, and Southern white men are mutually sharing the responsibilities of a constructive programme of education in the South which makes possible an active coöperation of the races in educational matters, which by many was not previously thought possible. The unique personnel of this Board, I have no doubt, was made possible as a result of the sentiment created by the Conference for Education in the South and the activities of the General Education Board.

It was through Doctor Frissell and Doctor Washington that this fund was established, and to them Miss Jeanes entrusted the responsibility for the organization of its Board. These gentlemen united in the selection of Dr. James H. Dillard, dean of Tulane University, New Orleans, as president, and associated with him were, of course, Doctor Washington and Doctor Frissell and such men as Mr. Andrew Carnegie, Bishop Abraham Grant of the A.M.E. Church; Chancellor David C. Barrow of the University of Georgia; Mr. Robert L. Smith, a Negro banker of Texas; Dr. Talcott Williams of the Pulitzer School of Journalism; Dr. Samuel C. Mitchell, then of the University of South Carolina and now president of Delaware College; Mr. George McAneny of New York; and Mr. J. Napier, lawyer and banker of Nashville, Tennessee. The Hon. William H. Taft, at that time Secretary of War, was also a member of the Board, and later, on becoming President of the United States, invited the Board to hold its annual sessions in the Cabinet room of the White House.

As secretary of the Board from the beginning, it was to me a source of continual encouragement to witness the fine spirit with which these men approached, not only the problems of education, but also the problems affecting the whole life of the Negro and the South. Following the death of Doctor Washington and Doctor Frissell, successively chairmen of the Executive Committee, it has fallen to my lot to discharge the duties of chairman.

When Doctor Dillard was asked to become president and general agent of the Foundation, there was considerable skepticism as to the wisdom of such a course, Doctor Dillard being a Southerner, born in Virginia, and for many years professor in a prominent educational institution in Louisiana. There was considerable doubt on the part of many whether the best interests of the coloured people would be served by the selection of such a man to become the executive officer of a movement designed especially to help in the educational development of the Negro. The history of the movement since that time has abundantly justified the wisdom of the choice. It would be hard to find a man anywhere in America who has displayed more tact, thoughtfulness, patience, and courage in dealing with the intricate and delicate problems that one must meet in striving to adjust race relations in the South than has Dr. James Hardy Dillard. Growing out of his activities with the Jeanes Fund, he was later asked to administer the John F. Slater

Fund, a similar foundation established earlier for the promotion of education among Negroes. The handling of these two funds has enabled him to touch large numbers of Negro school teachers in every part of the South, who are helped, encouraged, and inspired by his kindly and sympathetic, yet sober and efficient, approach to the problems of educating a race generally eager to learn, but often, like others, mistaken in its ideas of what education really means. He has had associated with him two men, one coloured and one white: Mr. W. T.B. Williams and Mr. B.C. Caldwell, both of whom have much the same spirit as Doctor Dillard himself. These three men have set an example for the entire country of the way in which it is possible for black and white men in the South to work together with entire self-respect and to win the respect, confidence, and appreciation of the people of both races.

Doctor Dillard from the beginning saw, what is becoming more and more evident to thoughtful workers among coloured people, that there can be no substantial and permanent improvement in the condition of the Negro in the South without a serious and sympathetic effort to create among Southern white people an intelligent interest in the condition and needs of the coloured people by whom they are surrounded and who form so important and indeed an indispensable part of the life of the South. The University Race Commission, composed of certain professors in each Southern State University, represents the practical application of these ideas in the most important educational circles of this section. These gentlemen for several years have conducted a serious and painstaking study of actual conditions existing among Negroes in their several localities, and have used the results of their study in connection with the university courses in sociology. Each year the Commission has issued a statement, setting forth the results and conclusions of the year's study, which is widely circulated in Southern publications, as well as in other parts of the country, and has had a strong influence in shaping the thought and opinion of educated men and women in the South toward the Negro.

Along with the movements already referred to, the Young Men's Christian Association has fostered a good plan under the direction of Dr. W.D. Weatherford whereby large classes in most Southern educational institutions have been organized; for the study of the race question, using textbooks prepared by Doctor Weatherford himself, and other literature issued by other organizations pertaining to this same subject. In support of this project the Phelps-Stokes Fund has established fellowships in certain of these institutions for the extended study of this question by young white men of university training, who are looking forward to a field of service in the larger development of the South. In many of these communities there has grown out of this movement a group of young college men who are dealing with the question, not only from a conventional, academic viewpoint, but by direct and immediate contact with welfare activities among Negroes in much the same way that led Dr. John Little of Louisville, Kentucky, and others of like spirit, to devote their lives to work among coloured people.

There have been among women also strong movements to bring about a larger sympathy and coöperation between the women of the two races in the South. It is not infrequent that coloured women are asked to address audiences of white women on this subject under the auspices of such organizations as the Young Women's Christian Association, state federations of women's clubs, and the women's auxiliaries of the various denominations. Few people know of the great service that Mrs. L.H. Hammond, as executive secretary of the Southern Publicity Committee, is rendering the general movement for inter-racial coöperation by putting before the public, through the Southern press, the hopeful, constructive things that white people and black people are doing together, thereby doing much to offset the wide publicity that is often given to instances of friction between individuals of the two races, which are by no means so common as the instances in which they coöperate.

I have not been officially connected with all of these movements, but it has nevertheless been my privilege and a source of much personal satisfaction frequently to be called into counsel concerning their plans and policies, and to interpret to the best of my knowledge not only the feelings of my own people, but also, what is sometimes more difficult, their desires and aspirations.

Most conspicuous perhaps among this type of activities is the Southern Sociological Congress, whose operations were made possible for a number of years through the interest and generosity of Mrs. Anna Russell Cole of Augusta, Georgia. This organization usually meets once each year, at which time an opportunity is given to representative white and coloured people for the free and candid discussion of any phase of the race question which the events of the year have brought into prominence. I have had the privilege of appearing before this Congress on more than one occasion, and I have been deeply impressed with the overall sincerity and sanity of its deliberations. Among its presiding officers have been men of the type of ex-Governor W. H. Mann of Virginia, Bishop Theodore D. Bratton of Mississippi, and ex-Governor B.W. Hooper of Tennessee. Its secretary from the beginning has been Dr. J.E. McCulloch, formerly of Nashville, who has been untiring in his efforts to make it a constructive force in furthering unselfish coöperation between the races.

More recent than any of these is a movement fraught with great possibilities for removing racial friction, organized in the city of Atlanta just before the close of the war by representative white men from all the Southern states under the leadership of a group of men among whom were Mr. John J. Eagan, a prominent banker of Atlanta; Dr. M. Ashby Jones, a Baptist minister of the same city; Dr. Wm. Louis Poteat, president of Wake Forest College in North Carolina; Dr. Robert H. McCaslin, a Presbyterian minister of Montgomery, Alabama; and Dr. Charles W. Crisler, of Mississippi.

In this movement a group of white men is working with a similar group of coloured men who together are quietly and effectively organizing like groups of both races in every state and county and city in the South. This movement is made possible by the financial assistance and coöperation of the War Work Council of the Y.M.C.A. The coöperation of such coloured men as President John Hope of Morehouse College, Atlanta; Prof. R.B. Hudson, secretary-treasurer of the National Baptist Convention; Mr. Harry H. Pace, secretary-treasurer of the Standard Life Insurance Company; Mr. Isaac Fisher, editor of the *Fisk University News,* and Dr. H. H. Proctor of the First Congregational Church, Atlanta. With such white men as I have mentioned above insures the vital character of the interest which these men have in the progress and development of the South. This group of substantial Southern men, in a way that is not true of any other of these movements, has organized with the avowed intention of securing for the Negro, in every community, fair and just treatment under the law as well as an equitable share in all those privileges and benefits for which he is taxed as a citizen. Though the movement is still in the early stage of development, definite results are already manifesting themselves.

In quite another way there is a tendency toward greater consideration, especially on the part of many large manufacturing establishments, for the welfare of their coloured employees. In these plants may be found what are known as "efficiency men," whose business it is to look after the morale of the coloured workers. The efficiency man has access at any time to the highest official of the plant, to whom he is directly responsible and to whom he is privileged to bring any matter pertaining to the welfare of these employees that in his judgment might increase their efficiency and thereby contribute to the advancement of the company's interests. I think now of the Tennessee Coal and Iron Company, with headquarters at Birmingham, Alabama, and establishments in other parts of the South, which has for some time employed Mr. Melvin J. Chisum at a comfortable salary, to render this kind of service for the company. He has the confidence of both the employee and the management, and this company has found that it is good business to have a strong, level-headed, and conscientious coloured man to deal directly with its coloured workers. I was told by the president of one establishment that such an official had reduced the friction by more than 50 per cent.; that the men were working much more regularly; and that the labour turnover or shifting had been similarly lessened.

Out of these organized movements there has grown up in almost every community a group of white and coloured men who coöperate in an unorganized way in the prevention of much misunderstanding and friction and the protection of the interests of the entire community. Coloured men coming from the North into these communities have often been surprised by the cordial way in which they have been received by prominent Southern men who have talked freely with them on many phases of this human problem.

I remember that Mr. Fred R. Moore, editor of the *New York Age,* not long ago visited many parts of the South and interviewed men of both races in many walks of life; among these was an ex-governor to whom Negroes outside of the local community would hardly have turned in their difficulties. He went into the interview prepared for almost anything, and was greatly surprised at the apparent cordiality with which he was received and the perfect candour with which they talked of the difficulties facing the races. Many other men are having similar experiences, all of which show the hopefulness of present-day events in the South. Twenty-five years ago such experiences would have been very rare, but today they are the rule rather than the exception.

But in many ways the most significant and substantial of these forward movements in the South, and one that is touching more people and vitalizing more interests than any other movement of its character, is the Rosenwald School-Building Project.

This movement began when Mr. Julius Rosenwald—one of America's most distinguished citizens and philanthropists, already referred to as one of our Tuskegee Trustees—put into the hands of Doctor Washington a sum of money sufficient to make an experiment in school building in six rural communities of Alabama. Doctor Washington felt that, with a few hundred dollars from outside sources, he could encourage the coloured people and induce the white people by private contributions and official appropriations to add to Mr. Rosenwald's gift a sum sufficient to erect and equip a modern one-teacher school building for Negroes in each of these communities. Mr. Rosenwald was so well pleased with the success of this experiment that at the present time he is providing a budget of something like $140,000 a year for the building of rural schools for Negroes in eleven Southern states. In four years 720 schools have been built under the supervision of Mr. C. J. Calloway, director of the Extension Department of Tuskegee Institute, at a cost of $1,133,083, of which sum $337,192 represents public appropriations; $88,445, private contributions from white people; $430,381, the gifts of coloured people; and $227,065, the gift of Mr. Rosenwald. It will thus be seen that the beneficence of Mr. Rosenwald has produced an additional sum of $906,018, all of which has gone directly into the providing of improved facilities for Negro education in the South.

Another result of the Rosenwald movement, larger and more important, is the awakened sense of greater responsibility for Negro education, not only on the part of public school authorities, but on the part of the Southern people in general for more adequate educational provision for Negroes. An indirect but no less significant result of the movement has been the added stimulus given to education in general in the South, which is bringing increased appropriations for this purpose in almost every community.

These Rosenwald schools are not merely school houses in the ordinary sense, but they are community centres from which influences radiate into all the avenues of Negro life, and where not infrequently both white and coloured people meet for the consideration of matters affecting the general welfare of the community. It was my privilege recently to share in such a gathering in north Alabama, where the principal of the white high school suspended the regular school work and brought his faculty and entire student body to the dedication of one of these Rosenwald schools, which had been recently completed through the united efforts of citizens of both races. It was one of the most interesting and helpful meetings in which it has been my pleasure to participate. The multiplying of such centres throughout the South, as Mr. Rosenwald is doing, is setting in motion a sentiment for inter-racial good will and coöperation, out of which there must ultimately come the larger freedom and greater justice for which all true Americans are striving.

I have taken some pains thus to recount certain forward-looking movements that are outstanding in their effect on our Southern life. In doing so I have not been unmindful of the injustice, discrimination, and unfair treatment which my people are all too often obliged to face to a greater or less extent in all parts of the country, but I am here trying to fix attention upon those strong and ever widening currents of constructive endeavour which move forward with a swiftness that accentuates the eddies of passion and prejudice which appear along their course.

In all the years of my experience, I have found that a great deal more is accomplished when one does not permit oneself to dwell too much upon the difficulties and discouragements which one encounters, but keeps constantly before one's mind those forces and influences which make for the removal of the very obstacles which often hamper one's progress. Knowing as I do the inner workings of these movements which I have described, and the character and spirit of the men behind them, I am satisfied that we have in them a force and an influence making for righteousness that cannot be defeated.

We all realize that the patient loyalty and self-denying devotion of the black man in America should have brought him more of the blessings and privileges of the civilization which his labour has helped to construct and his valour has helped to preserve. Nevertheless, in the forty years that have passed since I envied Sam Reed his place in the "big house" at "Pleasant Shade" and was unwittingly stung into reflection by my erstwhile friend, Ernest Morton, I have seen changes in the situation and condition of my own race, as well as in my own life, such as the most sanguine of that day —would hardly have predicted. Little did I think as I played with George Denney, the son of a Presbyterian minister on the red hills of Piedmont, Virginia, that forty years later I would be working in coöperation with Dr. George H. Denney, the president of the University of Alabama—he, among his people, training the youth of his race to a clearer understanding of and a broader sympathy with all humanity, and I, among my people, training, as best I may, the youth of my race to greater fortitude and a larger faith in themselves and in other selves.

And today I do not know of any work that offers larger returns, or more satisfactory results to conscientious endeavour, than the privilege that is granted to some of us to work with the people of our own race, in coöperation with men and women of other races, in the solution of these very human problems which all men have faced in one form or another in all ages of the world's history. And nowhere would I rather be found working than right here in Alabama, where the standards of such work have been set so high by a great soul of my own people, whose spirit still inspires the labours of both races in their efforts to bring men to that good will which is the highest hope of humanity.

Index

A. M. E. Church, 125
Adams, Lewis, 96, 97
advice, 37, 47, 79, 86, 92, 96, 97, 101, 109, 121
African Methodist Episcopal Church, 78
Alabama, 16, 27, 28, 51, 90, 94, 98, 101, 124, 128-132
Alderman, Edwin, 124
Alexander, Doctor, 2
Alexandria, Virginia, 24
Amelia County, Virginia, 1
America, 1, 2, 6, 62, 65-67, 71, 107, 115-118, 120, 124, 125, 131
American Expeditionary Force, 115, 116
American Negro, 66, 117
Anna T. Jeanes Foundation, 124
Appomattox River, 10, 47
Archambeau, John, 29
Armstrong, General, 20, 23, 26-29, 31, 43, 46, 49, 51, 53, 54, 57-62, 68-70, 72, 95, 99
army, 5, 11, 55, 58, 95, 108-111, 113
attitude, 4, 25, 39, 46, 54, 57, 66, 68, 73, 74, 86, 89, 94, 102, 107-109, 113, 122, 123
Attwell, E.T., 112

Baker, Ray Stannard, 118
Baldwin, Anna G., 23
Ballou, Col. C.C., 109, 110
Baltimore, Maryland, 23, 47, 69

Banks, Charles, 79
Barnett, Claude A., 100
Beacon Lights, 70
Bible Study, 24
Bible Training School, 113
Big Jack, 24
Birmingham, Alabama, 129
Blanton, Joshua E., 104
Blanton, Walker, 19
Boger, Henry H., 121
books, 9, 11, 12, 30, 31, 41, 42, 69, 70, 92, 126
Booth, Jennie D., 82
Bordeaux, 116
Bowen, Cornelia, 97
Bradford, Dr. Amory H., 71
Brandon, George, 75
Brent, Bishop, 114
Briggs, F. C., 23
Broad Brook Farm, 93
Brooklyn Bridge, 69
Brooklyn, New York, 50
Brown, Hugh M., 74
Brown, Lee, 13, 21
Bruyier, John, 51
Bullock, Judge W. S., 81
business, 23, 35, 36, 42, 51, 71, 73-76, 78-80, 90, 95, 96, 102, 103, 112, 113, 128, 129
Butler School, 22
Buttrick, Wallace, 75, 124

Cabaniss, George W., 109

Index

Caldwell, B.C., 126
Calhoun, R.C., 85
Calloway, C.J., 130
camp, 17, 18, 109, 110, 113, 114
Campbell, George W., 95, 96
Campbell, W. W., 89
Campbell, Wright W., 96
captain, 1, 5, 10, 16, 21, 46, 48, 54, 63, 70, 118
Carlisle School, 54
Carnegie, Andrew, 125
Carver, George W., 103
character, 5, 10, 39, 49, 55, 66, 76, 81, 90, 93, 114, 115, 128, 129, 131
Charlotte County, Virginia, 2
children, 2, 6, 10-12, 14, 22, 36, 37, 39, 40, 66, 77, 104, 123
Chisum, Melvin J., 129
churches, 12, 26, 37, 39, 43, 47, 69, 70, 78, 81, 87, 113
Civil War, 5, 22, 70, 94, 122
Claxton, P.P., 111
Cleveland, President, 43
Coates, Mary E., 31
Cole, Anna Russell, 127
college, 14, 28, 31, 44, 49, 70, 73, 97, 119, 124, 125, 127, 128
Collier, F. S., 65
committees, 19, 44, 49-51, 75, 89, 90, 108, 125, 127
conditions, 28, 29, 59, 66, 68, 79, 82, 92, 112, 114, 119, 126
conduct, 2, 30, 35, 53, 99, 108, 114, 115, 121
conferences, 34, 37, 73, 90, 110, 111, 116, 123-125
connections, 12, 18, 19, 31, 55, 75, 78, 83, 88, 101, 104, 108, 109, 111, 112, 114, 119, 121, 124, 126
consideration, 3, 27, 32, 44, 46, 89, 95, 111, 128, 130
conversations, 4, 8, 24, 58, 65, 85, 86, 116, 122
Cooper, Annie J., 74
coöperation, 44, 53, 59, 64, 68, 94-101, 106, 110, 114, 119, 124, 127, 128, 131, 132
Coppin, Fannie Jackson, 74
County School Board, 44
crime, 51, 67, 99, 113-116
Crisler, Charles W., 128
Crowder, John, 2
Cumberland County, 5, 35, 43, 44, 53, 58
Curtis, George L., 22, 46
Curtis, Mrs. J.L., 119
custom, 7-9, 15, 47, 49, 54, 82, 88
Cypress Baptist Church, 17

Danville, 89
Davis, J.E., 31
Day Nursery, 2
death, 2, 5, 9, 10, 14, 18, 60, 61, 64, 75, 77, 78, 81, 86, 101-105, 124, 125
Delaware College, 125
Democratic Party, 44
Denney, George H., 12, 131
department, 44, 50, 57, 88, 93, 100, 102, 103, 109, 110, 112, 113, 117, 119, 130
developments, 28, 37, 48, 53, 63, 64, 66, 68, 76, 78, 88, 96, 101, 102, 104, 117, 124, 125, 127, 128
Dillard, James H., 111, 125
Dinwiddie County, 18

Index

discipline, 20, 37, 39, 53, 57, 58, 63, 83, 91
Dismal Swamp, 24
district, 9, 11, 15, 19, 20, 35, 37, 38, 119
division, 109, 112, 115–118
DuBois, W. E.B., 115
Dunbar, Paul Laurence, 74
duties, 4, 7, 8, 13, 51, 54, 56, 59, 75, 84, 102, 111, 125

Eagan, John J., 128
East Indian, 81
education and learning:
    Gen. Armstrong's ideas on, 62
    classroom, 49, 54
    colleges, 14, 28, 31, 44, 49, 70, 73, 97, 119, 124, 125, 127, 128
    deficiencies of, 44, 47, 52
    effect of on blacks, 91, 97
    importance of for future, 15
    institutions for blacks, 26
    professors, 14, 126
    public school, 11, 130
    schooling, 17, 52, 91
    students, 6, 23–29, 31, 34, 41, 46, 47, 50, 52, 53, 54, 57, 58, 60–62, 64, 69, 71, 74, 75, 83, 91–93, 97, 99–101, 110
    teachers, 5, 6, 9, 11, 18, 23, 24, 27, 29–31, 34–41, 43, 44, 47–49, 51, 52, 54, 57, 58, 61, 62, 64, 65, 73–75, 82, 87, 91, 95, 97–102, 110, 121, 126, 130
    learning trades, 28
    university, 26, 74, 89, 94, 112, 123–128, 131
    Dr Washington's ideas on, 97

Edwards, George, 18
Edwards, William J., 97
Eggleston, J.D., 124
Europe and Europeans:
    Belgium, 65
    Britain, 124
    England, 30, 65, 69, 107, 124
    France, 65, 110, 113–121
    general, 65, 66
    Germany, 65, 107
    Ireland, 45, 65
    Italy, 65
    Poland, 13
    Switzerland, 65
Executive Board, 76
Executive Committee, 125
Extension Department, 88, 130
Extension Work, 72, 74, 75, 83
ex-slaveholders, 96
ex-slaves, 5

family, 4, 7–10, 12–14, 19, 24, 42, 86, 90
farms, 7, 8, 10, 12, 14, 15, 20, 22, 23, 27, 32, 35, 36, 66, 77, 85, 93, 124
Federal Army, 95
Federal Government, 22
First Congregational Church, 128
Fisher, Isaac, 128
Fisk University, 26, 97, 112, 128
Fisk University News, 128
Fitch, F. M., 75
Flippin, Norton, 44
food, 1, 2, 4, 38, 66, 77, 78, 80, 112, 114
Food Administration, 112, 114
Food Conservation, 78
Fort Des Moines, 109, 110

Fort Sill, 55
Fortress Monroe, 22, 55
Fourth Congressional District, 15
Freeland, Charles W., 46
friends, 7, 15, 17, 21, 24, 25, 29, 32, 35, 49, 54, 62, 65, 86, 87, 90, 94, 96, 99, 100, 105, 120
Frissell, Doctor, 56, 62, 64, 65, 68-71, 73, 74, 83, 84, 86-88, 90, 94, 99, 102, 105, 106, 125
Frissell, H. B., 24, 105, 124
fundraising, 64, 68, 69, 77, 83, 89, 92, 101, 125
Fusion Party, 18

Gandy, John M., 76, 101
General Education Board, 75, 124, 125
General Headquarters, 115, 116, 118
General Superintendent, 101
General War Time Commission, 113
Gibson, Charles H., 103
Gloucester County, Virginia, 75
Golden Slippers, 26
Golden Streets, 26
government and politics:
　democracy, 44, 76, 120
　elections, 38, 48, 64, 92, 106
　federal government, 22
　general, 17-19, 22, 32, 37, 38, 75, 107-113, 122
　institutions, 26, 68, 72, 74, 104, 110, 111, 113, 124, 126, 127
　social progress, 63
Grand Master, 75
Grant, Bishop Abraham, 125
Green, Rev. Anthony G., 36

Greencreek, 39
Gregg, James E., 106
Gresham, C.N., 74
groups, 17-19, 25, 27, 29, 39, 45, 58, 67, 68, 70, 86, 101, 106, 110, 111, 124, 127-129

Hall, Dorothy, 102
Hall, George C., 84
Hamilton, R.H., 97
Hammond, Mrs. L.H., 127
Hampden Sydney College, 124
Hampton Institute, 15, 20, 22, 23, 25-27, 30, 32, 34, 43, 57, 63, 65, 71, 72, 74, 75, 78, 82, 84, 88, 91, 94, 102, 104-106, 122, 124
Hampton Roads, 24, 56
Hardy, James, 125
hard-working, 24
Hare, C.W., 89
Harris, Elizabeth Hunt, 74
Harris, T.H., 111
Harrison, President, 44
Harvard Summer School, 65
Haynes, George E., 112, 113
health, 74, 76, 80, 84, 88, 93, 104
Holly Springs, 79
Holsey, Albon L., 111
Holtzclaw, W. H., 97
Hooper, B.W., 128
hope, 17, 49, 66, 82, 86, 105, 106, 109, 118-121, 123, 132
Hope, John, 111, 119, 128
hospital, 22, 84-86, 103, 105
House Father, 54
House, Col. E.M., 114
Howard University, 74
Howe, Albert, 41

Hudson, R.B., 128
Hunt, Nathan, 115
Hunton, Mrs. W. A., 119
Hyde, Elizabeth, 34
Hygeia Hotel, 61

ideas, 5, 12, 37, 38, 41, 46, 58, 62, 65, 73, 76, 79, 122, 123
Imes, Rev. G. Lake, 113
impressions, 9, 18, 19, 21, 24, 40, 80, 82, 89, 90, 98
inauguration of Tuskegee, 94
Indians, 24, 48, 54, 55, 58, 60, 62
Industrial Institute, 76, 100
injustice and inequity, 66, 92, 123, 131
instruction, 11, 16, 29, 31, 48, 56, 57, 64, 65, 83, 98
Irving, Judge Frank, 41

James River, 17, 18
James, Arthur Curtiss, 65
Jamestown, 12, 16, 32, 108
Jamestown Presbyterian Church, 12, 16, 32
Jeanes Fund, 125
Jesus Christ, 87
John A. Andrew Memorial Hospital, 103
Johnson, Katharine, 119
Jones, Beverley, 7
Jones, M. Ashby, 128
Jones, Thomas Jesse, 111, 115
Junior Class, 53
Junior Grade, 29

Kealing, H. T., 94
Kenney, Doctor, 86

Kenney, John A., 103
Knapp, Seaman A., 124
knowledge, 16, 17, 20, 30, 41, 73, 74, 76, 80, 83, 89, 92, 114, 127

Lakeland, Florida, 85
Langston, John M., 15, 38
Le Mans, 118
Lee University, 123
Liberty Bonds, 78
Liberty Loan, 114
Lippman, Captain Walter, 118
literature:
    books, 9, 11, 12, 30, 31, 41, 42, 69, 70, 92, 126
    newspapers, 23, 115
Little, John, 127
Logan, Adela H., 97
Long, Edgar A., 97
Lord, John, 70
Louisville, Kentucky, 127
Low, Seth, 88, 90, 93, 103, 104
Lower House of the State Legislature, 19
Ludlow, Helen W., 31
Lynchburg, 89

Macedonia Baptist Church, 32, 35
Mackie, Mary F., 30, 44
Macon County, 89, 98
Macon County Bank, 89
Mahone, General, 15
Mann, Governor, 76
Mann, W. H., 128
Mansion House, 60
Mason, Charles E., 88, 103
Mason, Mrs. Charles E., 103
master, 3–6, 21, 31, 72, 75, 87

Mastin, J.T., 77
McAneny, George, 125
McCaslin, Robert H., 128
McCulloch, J.E., 128
Mechanical Industries, 103
meetings, 12, 18, 21, 29, 55, 57, 69, 71, 75, 77, 78, 80, 100, 130
members, 2, 3, 10, 21, 40, 47, 48, 59, 62, 70-72, 75, 76, 78, 91, 92, 97, 112, 116, 123
Memorial Fund, 93
Metropolitan Museum, 70
Middle Class, 31
Middle Year, 29, 34, 46
Midway Baptist Church, 36
Military Instruction, 57, 83
Mill Creek, 22
Miller, Clyde R., 115
Miller, Kelly, 74
mind, 5, 10, 11, 25, 37, 43, 46, 53, 56-58, 64, 75, 84, 98, 105, 116, 131
Mississippi River, 69
Mitchell, Samuel C., 125
money, 16, 17, 18, 30, 31, 60, 64, 69, 77, 102, 120, 130
Montclair, New Jersey, 71
Montgomery, Alabama, 51, 90, 128
Montgomery, Isaiah T., 79
Moore, Fred R., 129
Moorland, J.E., 111
Morehouse College, Atlanta, 119, 128
Morrisette, John, 11
Mount Nebo, 39
Mount Vernon, 55
movements, 47, 78, 100, 105, 112, 122, 123, 126-129, 131
Munford, B.B., 124

Murphy, Edgar Gardner, 124
music, 25, 26, 81-83

Nashville, Tennessee, 125
Natchee, Paul, 55
National Army, 108, 109
National Baptist Convention, 128
National Guard, 109
National League on Urban Conditions, 112
National Negro Business League, 78, 96
Negro Democrats, 18
Negro Economics, 112
Negro Organization Society, 76-79, 84, 88
Negro Rural School Fund, 124
Negro Schools, 111
Negroes:
    as soldiers, 109-112, 114, 115, 118
    character of, 63, 65, 66, 73, 96, 116
    conscription and, 108, 109, 111
    criminality of, 113
    educational institutions for, 26, 72, 91, 95, 97, 105, 126, 130
    honours given to, 27
    in position of authority, 57, 73-76, 84
    in the press, 113
    Indians relationship to, 24, 48, 54, 55, 59, 60, 62-64
    loyalty to America, 107, 108
    military experiences, 53
    music of, 25, 26, 81
    officers' failures in France, 117, 118, 120
    politics and, 37, 38, 71, 129

prayer meetings, 12, 16, 26
reading and writing, 9
schooling of, 11
success of, 28
treating diseases of, 77
voting of, 18
whites' attitudes towards, 68, 70, 80, 95, 96, 123, 128
New England, 23, 30, 69
New Orleans, 125
New World, 25
New York, 50, 65, 69, 70, 79, 84, 88, 105, 109, 115, 124, 125, 129
New York City, 103
Norfolk, Virginia, 21
North Carolina, 24, 81, 128
Northern, 46, 54, 57, 59, 65, 71, 72, 82, 83, 89, 91, 94, 109, 123, 124

Ocala, Florida, 81
Ogden, Mrs. Robert C., 44
Ogden, Robert C., 44, 45, 54, 65, 123
Old Dominion Debating Society, 48
Old Point, 21, 22, 61
Old Roman World, 70
opportunity, 3, 5, 31, 50, 56, 57, 65, 83, 90, 91, 98, 105, 119, 120, 127
Organization Society, 76–79, 84, 88
organizations, 18, 48, 49, 75, 76, 78, 96, 116, 126, 127
overseers, 3, 4

Page, Inman, 74
Page, Walter H., 124
Palmer, Charlie, 38

Palmer, John H., 24
party, 1, 2, 15, 17–20, 38, 43, 44, 49, 53, 54, 60, 69, 72, 79, 88, 100, 115
Patterson, Thomas B., 25
Peabody, Francis G., 65
Peabody, George Foster, 109, 111, 124
Peace Conference, 116
Perkinson, Captain, 10
Perkinson, Pattie, 10
Pershing, General, 114, 117, 119
phases, 41, 42, 57, 68, 83, 85, 86, 93, 94, 101, 115, 118, 122, 129
Phillips, James H., 51
Piedmont, Virginia, 131
plantations, 2–5, 7, 8, 10, 11, 25, 32, 40, 41, 60, 83, 87
Plattsburg, New York, 109
Pleasant Shade, 7, 11, 14, 131
Postmaster General, 44
Poteat, Wm. Louis, 128
Pratt, Captain, 54
Presbyterian Church, 12, 16, 32
Prince Edward County, 2, 7, 18, 35, 41, 47
principal, 20, 24, 37, 59, 65, 72, 73, 77, 81, 89, 98, 99, 101–103, 105, 106, 108, 111, 121, 130
Proctor, H. H., 128
Protestantism:
    Baptists, 16, 17, 32, 35, 36, 39, 78, 128
    congregationalists, 71, 128
    Episcopalianism, 46, 78
    Methodists, 78
    Presbyterians, 5, 12, 16, 32, 128, 131
Public Instruction, 16

Index

Pulitzer School of Journalism, 125

racial, 59, 63, 64, 66, 67, 79, 94, 96, 127, 128, 131
Ramsey, Major Julius B., 103
Randolph, Agnes, 77
Readjuster Movement, 17, 18
Readjuster Party, 17, 19
Red Cross, 114, 116
Reed, Sam, 8, 131
Regular Army, 109, 110
Republican Party, 15, 43, 44
respect, 3, 18, 39, 60, 62, 95, 98, 99, 110, 111, 126
responsibility, 7, 31, 48, 58, 59, 83, 93, 98, 99, 101, 106, 120, 125, 130
Robert College (Constantinople), 49
Robert Hungerford School, 85
Roberts, Doctor, 84, 86
Robinson, Judge C.W., 90
Roman, Dr. C.V., 113
Roosevelt, Colonel, 88, 89
Rosenwald, Julius, 103, 129
Rosenwald, Mrs. Julius, 103
rural, 28, 38, 47, 58, 73, 75, 85, 112, 124, 130

Sailor Creek, 13
Saurez, M. E., 113
Savannah, Georgia, 46
saw-mill, 20, 23-25, 27, 29, 30, 63
Scarborough, W. S., 74
Scott, Emmett J., 85, 102, 110, 118
Scott, William M., 88, 103
Scottish Presbyterians, 5
Secession Movement, 43
self-possession, 120

self-reliance, 64
self-respect, 126
Senior Class, 34, 46-48, 69
serious-minded, 6
Sherman, M. J., 31
slaves:
    arrangements with masters, 4
    arrival in New World, 1
    overseers and, 3
    sale in auctions, 1
Smith, Robert L., 125
society, 48, 75-79, 84, 88
soldiers, 22, 53, 61, 106, 109, 111, 112, 114-116, 118-121
South America, 66
South Carolina, 81, 104, 125
Southall, Captain Frank, 16
Southern Army, 5, 11
Southern Publicity Committee, 127
Southern Sociological Congress, 127
Southern State University, 126
Southern Workman, 80
spirit, 14, 26, 56, 74, 87, 95, 97-100, 102, 106, 119, 125-127, 131, 132
Spurgeon, James R., 50
Standard Life Insurance Company, 128
State Board of Health, 76, 77
State Legislature, 19, 77
State Normal School, 15
states, 13, 50, 55, 56, 58, 67, 70, 75-78, 81, 82, 109, 111, 112, 114, 115, 124, 125, 128, 130
Stokes Foundation, 115
Stokes Fund, 111, 126
Student Army Training Corps, 113

Index

success, 8, 27, 43, 48, 57–59, 63, 76, 79, 89, 96, 100, 130
Summer School, 65
superintendent, 16, 20, 35, 36, 40, 41, 43, 44, 99, 101
Surry County, 17, 18
sympathy, 37, 61, 68, 87, 92, 95, 99, 106, 127, 131

Taft, William H., 125
Tampa, Florida, 84
Taylor, Robert R., 103
Temperance Society, 48
Tennessee Coal, 129
Thrift Stamps, 78, 114
Tillinghast, Mrs. I.N., 44
training, 9, 18, 26, 30, 41, 54, 69, 73, 82, 83, 97–99, 109, 113, 127, 131
traits of character:
    beauty, 26
    honesty, 98
    kindness, 3, 9, 24, 44, 85, 91
    wisdom, 51, 60, 97, 98, 106, 125
Trumbull, Frank, 88, 90, 103, 106
trustees, 65, 85, 89, 90, 92, 99, 103, 104, 106, 111, 130
Tuberculosis Society, 77
Tulane University, New Orleans, 125
Turner, H. B., 64, 75
Tuscaloosa, Alabama, 16
Tuskegee Institute, 24, 26, 28, 57, 71, 85, 89, 90, 92, 94, 97, 101, 103, 106, 108, 112–115, 119, 121, 130
Tuskegee Normal, 100
Tuskegee School, 95
Tuskegee Spirit, 97, 100, 108
Tuskegee Trustees, 130

U.S. Food Administration, 112
"Uncle Jim", 8
"Uncle Remus", 2
United States, 50, 55, 56, 58, 67, 111, 114, 115, 125
United States Army, 55, 56, 58, 111
United States Bureau, 115
United States Legation, 50
university, 26, 74, 89, 94, 112, 123–128, 131
"Up From Slavery", 30, 96
Urban League, 112

Vardaman, Governor, 80
Vassar College, 31, 44
Vaughan, Samuel, 7–12, 14, 19
Vaughan, William L., 32
Villard, Oswald Garrison, 111
Virginia Hall, 49
Virginia Legislature, 17
Virginia Polytechnic Institute, 14

Wake Forest College, 128
Waldron, Martha M., 31
Walthall, L.B., 35
Wanamaker, John, 54
war activities, 111, 116
War Camp Community Service, 113
War Department, 109, 110, 112, 117, 119
War Work Council, 128
Washington, Doctor, 30, 68, 71–73, 77, 79–82, 84–87, 89, 93, 94–103, 105, 106, 108, 110, 123, 125, 130
Washington, Major Allen, 63, 78, 111
Weatherford, W. D., 126

Wellesley College, 31
West Point, 109
West Virginia, 123
Western University, Quindaro, Kansas, 94
Westwood, William T., 29
White House, 125
Whiting, Joseph L., 112
Whittier Training School, 82
Wilberforce University, 74
Wilborn, A.J., 89
Willcox, William G., 85, 88, 94, 103
Williams College, 70
Williams, E.G., 77
Williams, Talcott, 125
Williamsburg, Virginia, 74
Wilson, President, 108, 110, 114, 121
Wilson, William L., 123
Womack, Captain, 5
women, 5, 9, 10, 23, 38, 49, 73, 74, 76, 79-81, 97, 100-102, 119, 124, 126, 127, 132
workers, 50, 72, 74, 75, 85, 93, 97, 98, 112, 118, 119, 126, 128, 129
world, 22, 25, 62, 67, 70, 87, 91, 92, 95, 98, 103, 118, 120
Wright, R.R., 74

Y.M.C.A., 85, 113, 118, 119, 128
Young, Col. Charles, 109
Young, N.B., 74

Zoölogical Gardens, 70

CPSIA information can be obtained at www.ICGtesting.com
Printed in the USA
267698BV00002B/28/A

SLOVER LIBRARY
NO LONGER PROPERTY OF
NORFOLK PUBLIC LIBRARY